D1463151

*The
Country House
in English
Renaissance
Poetry*

The Country House in English Renaissance Poetry

William A. McClung

University of California Press

BERKELEY·LOS ANGELES·LONDON

THE PUBLICATION of this book
has been aided by a grant from the
Hyder Edward Rollins fund.

Photographic Acknowledgements

1, 2, 3, 5, 6, 7, 9, 10, 11, 12, 15, 19, 20, 23,
24, 26, 31—*Country Life*   4, 21, 25, 28,
29—A. F. Kersting   8—by courtesy of the
Marquess of Salisbury   13, 14, 17—The
Trustees of Sir John Soane's Museum
16—Ian Dunlop   22, 27—Royal
Commission on Historical Monuments
(Crown Copyright)   30—British Crown
Copyright, reproduced with permission of
the Controller of Her Britannic Majesty's
Stationery Office   34—J. A. Booth

University of California Press
Berkeley and Los Angeles, California

University of California Press, Ltd.
London, England

Copyright © 1977 by
The Regents of the University of California

ISBN 0-520-03137-7
Library of Congress Catalog Card Number:
75-27928
Printed in the United States of America

Contents

List of Illustrations

List of Illustrations

Preface

*T*HE PUBLICATION in recent years of several distinguished studies of the English country house prompts me to acknowledge their importance, and to point out that my subject is primarily Renaissance poetry and domestic architecture. Richard Gill's *Happy Rural Seat: The English Country House and the Literary Imagination* (Yale, 1972) examines the estate in English fiction since Henry James (while briefly surveying earlier literature); Alastair Duckworth's *The Improvement of the Estate* (Johns Hopkins, 1971) is confined to Jane Austen. In a penetrating analysis of the societal myths unconsciously nourished by celebrations of rural life, Raymond Williams, in *The Country and the City* (Oxford, 1973), examines Jonson, Carew, and Marvell in several closely packed pages.

For over seventy-five years *Country Life* has performed an invaluable service in presenting splendidly illustrated scholarly studies of the great houses of England. Those articles (particularly by Christopher Hussey), and the work of Sir John Summerson, Sir Nikolaus Pevsner, and Mark Girouard, are points of departure for anyone interested in the English country house as an architectural as well as a literary phenomenon. Paul Cubeta's extremely useful "A Jonsonian Ideal: 'To Penshurst',", *Philological Quarterly*, XLII, No. 1 (January, 1963), not otherwise cited by me, is an important examination of the literary motifs of that poem.

I conceived the idea of writing about the literary significance of the English country house in 1968, while a student in Harry Levin's seminar on Utopia and the Golden Age, at Harvard. It occurred to me then that the nostalgic backward glances cast by English poets of the Renaissance both illuminated and misrepresented the vigorous native tradition of manorial architecture. Professor Levin and Professor Reuben Brower helped this notion evolve into a dissertation and then into this book. My debt to them is enormous, and in the case of Professor Brower, who died in 1975, unpayable.

A Dexter Fellowship from Harvard made it possible for me to visit the houses that had begun to fascinate me; a grant from Mississippi State University helped in acquiring suitable photographs. I am grateful to Stephen Orgel for the pains he took in reading the manuscript and for the unfailing intelligence and suitability of his advice; my namesake at the University of California Press, William J. McClung, has been equally generous with his time and perceptive in his recommendations; and Ulrich Knoepflmacher gave particular assistance on several points.

The Marquess of Exeter was kind enough to show me around parts of Burghley House usually closed to the public; I am glad to thank him again. To Kenneth Bleeth I owe a special debt of gratitude; I count on him to collect it.

W. A. McC.

Introduction

*T*HE SMALL group of seventeenth-century poems that
make up the genre of English country-house poetry stands
near the head of a tradition of praise of the decorum and
plenitude of the English manorial estate. In its period of
greatest flowering under Victoria and Edward VII, the
country house figured heavily in English fiction; and by
the 1920s Yeats could present images of splendid secular
order in terms of the architecture and gardens of the
recent past. "Ancestral Houses" is, of course, elegiac;
Waugh's novels as well, particularly *A Handful of Dust*,
bitterly assault the destroyers of the old manorial ways.
Yet the complaint is not new. Before 1612, Ben Jonson
made the decay of country living a thesis of "To Penshurst," and Martial, fifteen hundred years before him,
has something similar to say. In each case what might
more prosaically be called a large farm has served as the
locus of a great number of social and ethical norms. In the
continual failure of "modern" society to live up to the
virtues implicit in the life of the traditional manor estate,
the poet and the critic find their double text: praise of the
enduring values of the country house, and criticism of the
men who subvert them.

Even in its origins, in Jonson's poems and in earlier
verse in praise of rural living, the note of anger, fear, and
bitterness is struck. To understand what the English
country house meant to those Stuart and Commonwealth
poets who first memorialized it in verse of some length
and seriousness, one must look at some of the buildings
themselves, not only the ones praised, like Penshurst
Place and Appleton House, but also the anonymous

1

objects of the poets' dislike—the house, for example, that is Penshurst's foil, "built to envious show / Of touch, or marble . . ."

For the great country houses of the late sixteenth and early seventeenth centuries, which are precisely those "proud, ambitious heaps" that Jonson despises, were the creations of powerful noblemen, the *arrivistes* of Elizabeth's and James's reigns. These men, whose base of power was at Court, built, in the full tide of their success, lavish country houses in their home counties. These estates were not centers of power, on the model of the feudal seigniory, but creations of it, made possible by the immense wealth gained from political and financial sinecures at Court. The roll of their builders is a list of the political and financial magnates of the age: William Cecil, lord Burghley, architect of Elizabeth's policy and builder of Burghley and Theobalds; Sir Christopher Hatton, whose house at Holdenby was the largest in England; Robert Cecil, earl of Salisbury and Lord High Treasurer, master of Hatfield; Thomas Howard, earl of Suffolk, builder of Audley End. The names, like the buildings, are of great weight.

But though some of these men are elsewhere the objects of poets' praise, their houses—the most important architectural ventures in England before the early seventeenth century—are not. A step beneath the Tudor "new men" and their families, at least in terms of power and riches, were a number of wealthy landed public servants, whose manor estates typified to Jonson and his circle the values of a settled and responsible gentry. The Sidneys at Penshurst Place in Kent, the de Greys (earls of Kent) at Wrest in Bedfordshire, and the Crofts, who held Saxham in Suffolk, were ancient families prospering under the Tudor and Stuart regimes; and Sir Lewis Pemberton, whose house, Rushden, in Northamptonshire had been visited by James I, was not far beneath them. Holding manors of considerable antiquity, they made extensive, even lavish additions and renovations to meet the demands of Elizabethan and Jacobean standards of luxury, yet their houses appeared modest by comparison with the gigantic new mansions rising around them.

The subjects of the poems in the country-house genre are both the old families and their houses, and it is within the framework of the routine of manorial labor and manorial hospitality—"housekeeping," as it was called— that the poet finds the subject of his praise. Marvell's Lord Fairfax, whose house at Nunappleton is the last to be so memorialized, was, perhaps even more than the Sidneys, an important character in English history; he shares with his Jacobean and Caroline predecessors the honors of distinguished public service.

The estates of these men share the honors as well, and are throughout the genre contrasted to their advantage with the architecture of the great house-builders of the age. In praising houses like Wrest and Penshurst, the poets stress many traditional manorial customs; in the routine and economy of the household they find these customs, which they take to be central to the health of English society, both respected and renewed, day by day. In the newer sort of country houses they see a fall off from the good old ways, and in their eyes modern architecture—indeed, Architecture itself—is much to blame.

To praise by negation, to conclude that the antique is precious because the modern is debased, would not be sufficiently convincing. To define the virtues of the traditional English manor, Jonson, Herrick, Carew, and Marvell draw upon several sources, recent and remote, of popular and literary sentiment on the subject. Praise of rural living in its simplest form was familiar to English poets in poetry as old as Hesiod's *Works and Days* and as contemporary as Joseph Hall's book of satires, *Virgidemiae,* of 1598. Both in the immediate background and in the classical sources, however, a steady gradation can be traced from full elaboration of the praise of a country house, in Martial's Epigram III, 58 ("Baiana nostri villa, Basse, Faustini"), back to the origins of the myth of the virtues of country living in the classical myth of the Golden Age. Motifs of primitive, rural, and pristinely ancient country life infuse the praise of the seventeenth-century English manor, and Roman satirical assaults on the decay of manorial and urban hospitality find their way directly into Jonson's poems.

The existence of the genre was established by G. R. Hibbard, who pointed out the six poems that may fairly be said to comprise it: Jonson's "To Penshurst" and "To Sir Robert Wroth," Herrick's "Panegerick to Sir Lewis Pemberton," Carew's "To Saxham" and "To My Friend G. N., from Wrest," and Marvell's "Upon Appleton House."[1] But the context, architectural and social as well as literary, is much more my subject than Hibbard's, for both the shaping influence of classical literature and the continuity of specific architectural and literary motifs in the six poems themselves remain largely unexamined.

In Chapter 1 I shall take up the metamorphosis of the Hesiodic story of the Golden Age into a myth of the

1 "The Country House Poem of the Seventeenth Century," *Journal of the Warburg and Courtauld Institutes,* XIX (1956), 159–74. The article is reprinted in *Essential Articles for the Study of Alexander Pope,* ed. Maynard Mack (Hamden, Conn.,1964). Other material relating solely to the genre includes Charles Molesworth's "Property and Virtue: The Genre of the Country-House Poem in the Seventeenth Century," *Genre,* I, 2 (April, 1968), 141–57, and "In More Decent Order Tame: Marvell, History, and the Country-House Poem," (diss., State University of New York at Buffalo, 1968).

fruitful and beneficent country villa; in Chapter 2 I shall look at the historical and literary backgrounds of country-house life and the country-house poem in England up to Jonson's time. Chapter 3 will argue that the Elizabethan and Jacobean prodigy houses are the "proud, ambitious heaps" of "To Penshurst" and the later poems. Chapter 4 is an analysis of the contributions of Jonson, Herrick, and Carew to the genre; the poems are discussed as though they were variants upon a single, *ur*-country-house poem, and I shall examine them according to generic motifs. Marvell, and several later poets, deform Jonson's model to such a degree that they will have a chapter to themselves. With them, the genre comes to an end.

A formal analysis of the country-house genre should not obscure the essentially didactic impulse behind these metrical critiques, an impulse well sketched by Hibbard and one natural to poets for whom, as for most men of the seventeenth century, the country possessed great moral prestige. The hierarchical society of a European manor was the unit and model of the earlier medieval state and its agricultural function fundamental to the existence of men. Little remained of such a society in seventeenth-century England except a stubborn belief on the part of many poor and well-off alike that it was, or had been, a divinely ordained way of life that was in a state of decay. The extent to which the life of a country estate meant different things to different men during this period of change is interestingly caught by Tolstoy, in wholly alien circumstances:

> To Constantin Levin the country was the background of life—that is to say, the place where one rejoiced, suffered, and laboured, but to Koznyshev the country meant on one hand rest from

work, on the other a valuable antidote to the corrupt influences of town, which he took with satisfaction and a sense of its efficacy. To Levin beyond all the country was good because it was the scene of labour, of the usefulness of which there could be no doubt. To Koznyshev the country was particularly good because there one could and should do nothing.[2]

We are perhaps accustomed, because of our very urban lives, to value the country as Koznyshev appreciates it. In the estate poems of Jonson and his imitators—as well as of Martial—we deal with a productive manor-farm, and we might seek its contemporary equivalent rather in the large ranches of Texas or California than in either a Biltmore or a lodge in the north woods.

2 *Anna Karenin,* trans. Rosemary Edmonds (London, 1954), p. 257.

1

The Origins
of the Country-House Genre
in the Myth of the Golden Age

ARCHITECTURE, which appears in such a poor light in "To Penshurst," shared in Jonson's time the ambiguous status of all the artisan crafts, denounced by Seneca in the long *Ninetieth Epistle* as effects of man's historical degeneration from the condition of the Golden Age. The legend so well examined by Harry Levin in *The Myth of the Golden Age in the Renaissance* need not be surveyed again, but its most important motif, that of the earth's free giving of her bounty (*sponte sua*, in Ovid's phrase), finds its way into the moral and domestic economy of the English country house. Hesiod's tale of how men who are by nature good lived in rapport with a benevolent planet contributes to a much more recent mythology that sets virtuous and fruitful country estates in opposition to vicious and sterile ones. Along the route of translation from Hesiod to Ben Jonson lie Juvenal's satires on inhospitable hosts and Martial's epigrams on life in town and country, and around the Roman poets a rich literature in verse and prose on the subject of man's askewed relationship with the natural world.

Ovid gave the myth of the metallic ages of man's existence its fixed form in the *Metamorphoses*, and placed the origin of both agriculture and architecture in the degenerate Silver Age (I, 121–24). But Vergil's role in the development of the myth is more important for the history of the praise of country life. In the *Georgics,* which glorify husbandry, he colors his contemporary Italian farmers with golden hues, reminding us that Astraea, the tutelary deity of the golden men, dwelt last among farmers before leaving earth for good. Emphasis thus shifts from the necessary evil of rural labor to its beneficial and virtuous nature. Vergil reinforces the echo of the Golden Age by rewarding his farmers' harsh toil with the spectacular abundance of a soil that meets them halfway (II, 458–60). Amid the peaceful fields, many Golden-Age *topoi*—for example, freedom from war and from seafaring—seem to survive undamaged. But if the plow is redeemed, the cottage is not: Vergil sets country in opposition to city life, and finds in architecture—the "foribus domus alta superbis" (II, 461)—the manifestation of pride, avarice, greed, and other vices from which his husbandmen are free.

Sentiment about the happy life of the peasant was familiar to the Renaissance through Horace's second epode, "Beatus ille qui procul negotiis," which Jonson translated. But the praise of country living, though reposing upon a tradition of idealized labor, easily graduated upwards, in both classical and modern literature, to admiring descriptions of well-heeled estate life. Horace himself, rusticating on his Sabine farm, enjoyed days of conversation, entertainment, and rest, contrary to a life of affairs in Rome (Satire II, 6). Martial's picture of a day in the life of the master of a villa ("De Rusticatione") includes activities appropriate only to the owner of a fairly large estate: "At daybreak I pray to the gods; I visit my servants and afterwards my fields, and to my staff I assign their proper tasks":

luce deos oro; famulos, post arva reviso,
partibus atque meis iustos indico labores.

A life governed by the routine of "lunch, drink, sing,
play, bathe, dine, go to bed"[1] may imply that rural
activities are fundamental, having an excellence or right-
ness about them absent from city activities; at the same
time the portrait of a landowner's day is realistic. It is
perfectly possible to admire the life of a peasant, like
Claudian's Old Man who never left the neighborhood of
Verona, but the enjoyment of cultivated tastes and of the
privileges of ownership can be assimilated to the rural
ideal.

To a greater or lesser degree, each poem of the six in
the English estate genre takes up the theme of hospitality,
or its opposite, usually in an insistent manner. Jonson set
the pattern, finding his model not in Martial's epigram on
Faustinus' house but in a group of poems that fall within
the convention of the attack on the contemporary viciousness of life in the city, that is, in Rome. For life in
Rome is, according to the remarkably consistent opinions
of the Latin moralists, vulgar, savage, and degrading; and
Martial, Juvenal, and Pliny unite in specifying the
custom of serving unequal fare at the table as the emblem
of the collapse of an antique system of largesse and, one
might fairly say, charity.[2] Ben Jonson's experience at

1 *Martial: Epigrams,* trans. Walter C. A. Ker, Loeb Classical Library
(Cambridge, Mass., and London, 1950), II, 521. Subsequent translations from Martial are from this edition.
2 In Epistle II, 6, Pliny criticizes stinginess at a banquet, a
contemporary kind of viciousness ("istam luxuriae et sordidum
novum societatem"). He speaks of a dinner party at which he and his
host had the best things to eat, lesser guests ate inferior food, and
clients of both had poorer fare still. A dinner, Pliny insists, presupposes
equality among diners.

Theobalds in 1607, when Lord Salisbury served his guests a meal different from (and presumably inferior to) that which he served himself, must have stimulated his memory of Martial's Epigram III, 60. "Why do I dine without you, Ponticus, although I am dining with you?" asks Martial, who observes that his host eats "a turtle-dove with bloated rump," while he has a "magpie that has died in its cage":

> aureus inmodicis turtur te clunibus implet,
> ponitur in cavea mortua pica mihi.

Drummond records Jonson's response, at Lord Salisbury's table, to his host's inquiry why "he was not glad": "My Lord said he yow promised I should dine with yow, bot I doe not."[3] And the incident finds its way into "To Penshurst," lines 61–66.

Such situations were apparently common in Rome, and both Martial and Juvenal link them with the vulgarity of new money. Gourmandism arouses Martial's disgust in an epigram (X, 31) about men who sell their slaves for the price of a superb fish. Juvenal, in the Fourth Satire, derides the purchase of a mullet for 6,000 sesterces. In the Fifth Satire, against the parvenu Virro and his vulgar dinner party, Juvenal suggests the social consequences of such behavior. His indignation is coupled with deep sense of humiliation; the indignation finds its way into Herrick's poem to Pemberton, where the niggardly servants and disgusting fare served to Virro's less favored guests in Rome reappear with the realism of the comic stage. But the deep sense of shame felt by Juvenal, a poet, man of letters, and free citizen, at his reduction to the status of an inferior strongly impressed Jonson. Virro's

3 Jonson, *Complete Works,* ed. C. H. Herford and Percy and Evelyn Simpson (Oxford, 1925–52), I, 141. Hereafter cited as H & S.

avarice prompts his denial of fine food to others; hospitable largesse is the great virtue of Penshurst. Virro's sadism leads him to humiliate the gentleman of modest means; Lord Sidney (Lord Lisle after 1605) receives Jonson as an equal. "Olim maior habebatur donandi gloria": once, Juvenal affirms, it was better to share than to hoard. That *olim*, that former age, in Jonson's eyes as in Juvenal's is the Golden Age of hospitality.

Athenaeus tells us that the Arcadians dined communally, masters with slaves;[4] Martial praises a friend, Licinianus, around whose rustic hearth slaves and strangers mix freely with the Master (I, 49); and in Ben Jonson's translation, Horace speaks of "The wealthy household swarme of bondmen met, / And 'bout the steeming chimney set" (Herford and Simpson, VIII, 291). In the ideal dinner party of his Satire II, 6, Horace exclaims, "O noctes cenaeque deum," "when before my own Lar we dine, my friends and I, and feed the saucy slaves from the barely tasted dishes." The country folk who pour into Sir Robert Wroth's Hall at Durrants benefit from this admittedly special relaxation of degree, a communality recalling both some distant earlier time, even the Golden Age, and the familial nature of the entire manorial family.

A "family" expanded to dozens, even hundreds, of souls can supply all its own needs. Vergil stresses the benefits of "unbought provisions," the products of one's own farm and garden (*Georgics*, IV, 132–33). The theme is echoed in Juvenal and Martial, speaking of enjoyable meals where the table is supplied by the master's own estate (Satire XI; Epigrams I, 55, and X, 48). Such meals

4 *Athenaeus: The Deipnosophists*, trans. Charles B. Gulick, Loeb Classical Library (Cambridge, Mass., and London, 1951–57), II, 183. Statius writes of a similar meal (*Silvae*, I, 6).

recreate the glorious past in the corrupt present and anticipate the communal meals at Penshurst, Durrants, Wrest, Rushden, and Saxham. The medieval manor was very nearly self-sufficient, as was its not remote descendant, the eighteenth-century Virginian plantation. Their contrary is the house that Jonson sets in opposition to Penshurst—a newer sort of country house, whose gorgeous façade was reared at the expense of the countryside and stands in opposition to it.

In a villa at Formiae, a seaside resort, Martial found such a harmony between the estate supplying provisions and the master using and distributing them (Epigram X, 30). He conflates motifs from the myth of the Golden Age with the list of rural pleasures and activities. The calm waters, the refreshing coolness, and the "assisting air" set the scene, but nature herself is actively benevolent. "The line seeks not its prey in the distant sea, but the fish, descried from above, draws down the cord cast from bed or couch" (lines 16–18). The *sponte sua* motif of the golden age *topos* here animates the fish, who volunteer themselves as food for a leisurely fisherman. The motif of "unbought provisions" also characterizes the villa at Formiae; the table is "self-supplied" from the fishpond, where, when the master calls, "bidden to appear, aged mullet put forth their heads."

In the system of the golden world, nature serves man with the necessities and even the luxuries he requires; but in the modern world, and in the city, he must struggle for survival. At the villa at Formiae all comes of its own accord, without coercion. One compels nothing, and one is therefore cleared of the taint of greed, or of the necessity to be a predator. As Tibullus writes of the Golden Age, "with milky udders came the ewes unbidden to meet the carefree swain" (Elegy I, 3).[5] Such a state of things concurs with the absence of war, private property, and other conditions that we call "necessity." In characterizing a seaside villa in the particular language of this myth, Martial transfers to a rural household the idea of the "great good place."

But in the Golden Age there were no houses, much less well-staffed villas. Vergil praises his fortunate rustics by dissociating them from the splendid houses of cities, where greed, luxury, vanity and other traits linked with the decay from the first age are in evidence. Seneca's axiom in the Ninetieth Epistle that "men cease to possess all things the moment they desire all things for their own"[6] leads to an attack on all crafts, especially architecture; the idea is a Roman commonplace. Even Varro and Columella, both of whom offer practical descriptions for building a large country villa, the seat of a working estate or manor, are careful to place themselves on the side of antique simplicity. It would surprise Palladio to know that beauty or even splendor of decor should interfere with the efficiency of a country house; but Varro (B.C. 116–27), criticizing a new "frescoed" villa, deplores the contemporary desire for splendid apartments.[7] The ancients built to answer utility, the moderns luxury. Columella, in the following century, describes the tripartite Italian villa revived in the sixteenth century by Palladio;

5 *Catullus, Tibullus, and Pervigilium Veneris,* trans. J. P. Postgate, Loeb Classical Library (Cambridge, Mass., and London, 1956), p. 207.

6 *Seneca ad Lucilium Epistulae Morales,* trans. Richard M. Gummere, Loeb Classical Library (Cambridge, Mass., and London, 1953), II, 397.

7 *Cato, On Agriculture; Varro, On Agriculture,* trans. William D. Hooper and Harrison B. Ash, Loeb Classical Library (Cambridge, Mass., and London, 1954); for Varro's comments see p. 215.

13

it is a comfortable enough place, with winter and summer apartments, baths and promenades, but by his definition it is simple and conforms to antique plainness.[8]

Thus even two practical agricultural treatises are in part informed by the notion that now the problems of architectural splendor and material luxury are getting out of hand. This sense of something having gone too far, and more specifically of urban vices infecting the countryside, is strongly felt throughout Martial's epigram to Bassus, and ultimately in Jonson as well.[9] Martial's poem is addressed to Bassus, the proprietor of a frescoed villa or "pictam villam" in Martial's words. It is set in a garden of "idle myrtle-beds and widowed planes and clipped clumps of box":

> . . . otiosis ordinata myrtetis
> viduaque platano tonsilique buxeto
> (lines 2–3)

or, in other words, a formal garden of some pretensions. Called a town-house away from town ("domus longe"), the villa of Bassus takes on the characteristic idleness, unproductivity, and vanity of city dwellings, for one reason because the garden takes up otherwise fruitful soil ("ingrata lati spatia detinet campi"). It is a big house with a belvedere over the garden ("turre ab alta prospicis meras laurus"). But the villa produces nothing. Even staples have to be purchased at the market in town:

8 *On Agriculture,* trans. Harrison Boyd Ash, E. S. Forster, and Edward H. Heffner, Loeb Classical Library (Cambridge, Mass., and London, 1948–55).

9 Besides the poem on Bassus' and Faustinus' houses, Martial wrote epigrams criticizing useless domestic display (I, 55) and fancy but uncomfortable modern houses (XII, 50).

et vinitorem farre pascis urbano
pictamque portas otiosus ad villam
holus, ova, pullos, poma, caseum, mustum.

(lines 48–50)

"The villa of our friend Faustinus, at Baiae," is quite
another thing. Honest and artless, this working farm
("rure vero barbaroque") is alive with animals. Bulls roar,
steers fight, and birds strut about; while pigs follow the
bailiff's wife around, "the tender lamb waits for its dam's
full udder." It is a real farm. The household is made up of
servants who go about their emblematically useful
tasks—"the unkempt pruner" who "brings home late
grapes," the woman feeding pigs, and the wine-seller who
"does not idly sicken with pale-faced ease." The slaves, in
fact, love their work and do not have to be goaded; they
rise to the occasion. "The kindly garden keeps the town
slaves cheerfully busy, and, without the overseer's order,
even the wanton long-curled pages gladly obey the bailiff;
even the delicate eunuch delights in work":

exercet hilares facilis hortus urbanos,
et paedagogo non iubente lascivi
parere gaudent vilico capillati,
et delicatus opere fruitur eunuchus.

(lines 29–32)

Reverence for the household gods completes the harmonious tableau.

The villa generates good will in the countryside.
Visitors, presumably tenants and inferiors, come with
useful gifts of cheese, honey, meat, and game, "and the
strapping daughters of honest farmers ("grandes proborum virgines colonorum") offer in a wicker basket their

mother's gifts" (lines 39–40). Guests of higher rank are received as well: "When work is done a cheerful neighbor is asked to dine; no niggard table reserves a feast for the morrow; all take the meal, and the full-fed attendant need not envy the well-drunken guest."

> facto vocatur laetus opere vicinus;
> nec avara servat crastinas dapes mensa,
> vescuntur omnes ebrioque non novit
> satur minister invidere convivae.
>
> (lines 41–44)

In contrast, "elegant starvation" ("famem mundam") is the rule at the villa of Bassus.

The description of the villa of Faustinus praises both absolutely and by comparison. In contrast with Bassus' house, the Baian villa has no unpleasant attendants, nor is hospitality stinted. It is not actually stated that Bassus is such a poor host, but that would seem to be one point of the admonitory nature of the epigram. More important is the degree to which Faustinus' establishment incorporates the spontaneity of the Golden Age. Everyone performs his task of his own accord, and the riches of the earth grace the villa. The spontaneous overflow of generosity takes the form of traditional hospitality, which is returned and renewed by the neighboring farmers. Bassus' world is a complete and closed system, in which the traditional virtues of country life are realized in the framework of a large, hierarchical villa. The *sponte sua* theme is one of the Golden Age *topoi*; it has been applied to vegetables, to animals, and now, most strikingly, to men. The slaves, tenants, free farmers, and neighbors of equal rank all participate in this cheerful agricultural economy; it is a moral economy as well and depends, by implication, upon the good sense of the master, Faustinus himself. In the workaday routine of a great Italian farm, Martial finds the key characteristics of rich productivity, unforced harmony, and overflowing generosity that are the touchstones of the Hesiodic and Ovidian myth.

Architecture remains under a shadow. It is perhaps left for us to assume that the Baian villa "stands an ancient pile." Doubtless it would have pleased Varro, but it is not, as a structure, of interest to Martial. Architectural descriptions are limited to details of the other house, descendant of the "superba civium potentiorum limina" of Horace's Second Epode. So it is for Jonson: his architectural vocabulary is largely a vocabulary of attack.[10]

10 Statius wrote poems in praise of two lavish country houses, one at Tivoli (*Silvae,* I, 3), and one at Sorrento (*Silvae,* II, 2). In both he inverts Martial's arguments and praises the luxury and artifice of the villas. Apollinaris Sidonius, the fifth-century poet and bishop, wrote a long poem in praise of the Burgus Pontii Leontii, a fortified manor near Bordeaux. Although Statius' influence is clear, the paean adds to its description of fine apartments a mythological account of the founding of Pontius Leontius' house, and praise of the wife and descendants of the master.

2

The Background of the Country-House Poem in England

The Genre and Modern Historians

*T*HE ENGLISH genre of country-house verse includes poems that memorialize particular estates, rather than pieces of landscape; the houses are not necessarily described. G. R. Hibbard has outlined the characteristics of the genre in terms of the objects of the poet's praise: building and grounds, gardens, fields and meadows, the master's virtue, his charity to his dependents, and his hospitality to friends (the poet among them) and to strangers. Each motif does not occur in every poem, but in general those introduced are subsumed under a larger argument: the comparison of the estate in question with a less desirable type of country house. The virtues of the old, honorable, and productive manor shine in comparison with the meretricious architecture and cold inhospitality of the new one.

The six poems central to the genre are Jonson's "To Penshurst" and "To Sir Robert Wroth," Herrick's "A Panegerick to Sir Lewis Pemberton," Carew's "To Saxham" and "To My Friend G. N. from Wrest," and Marvell's "Upon Appleton House." Joseph Hall's Satire V, 2, is an important, and I believe hitherto unnoticed, source. Charles Cotton's lines on Chatsworth in *The Wonders of the Peake,* though they are part of a larger poem and depart from the traditional assumptions of the genre, can be included as well; and Pope's *Epistle to Burlington* and *Epistle to Bathurst* are indebted to Hall's Satire and to the genre.

Hibbard has offered an explanation of the architectural and social background of the poems. Penshurst he takes to be, in Jonson's eyes, the type of the medieval English manor; its "household" is of the medieval communal kind. The "envious show" of the newer sort of country house is interpreted to mean the Italian Renaissance, or Palladian architecture of Inigo Jones and his followers. The social significance of such a change in house design is explained by a reading of English history that interprets Jonson's age as the time of the rise of Protestant individualism, capitalism, and Puritanism—the three closely linked—and hence as the time of the destruction of "medieval" or feudal ties of obligation. Charity, in the form of hospitality or "housekeeping," as it was known, is said to be one of the victims of this change in the national character, and the country-house poets, aware of the situation, argue the case of an older, conservative humanism.

The kinds of buildings that might have seemed traditional or newfangled to Jonson will be examined in the next chapter. But although "To Penshurst" was probably written no later than 1612,[1] the buildings that have made Jones's reputation as a great innovator in English architecture were at that time years short of completion, or even of being commissioned, and it is highly unlikely that Jonson can be speaking of him.

1 H & S, XI, 33.

Nevertheless, Hibbard's interpretation has not been questioned.

The dubious identification of Jonson's "touch, or marble" is important because it has been tied into the accepted explanation for the apparent decay of housekeeping. By linking Jones and his Continental style to the growth of economic individualism, Hibbard and others put the English poets in the position of defenders of an indigenously English and feudal society. But the nature of the historical movements of the time is very much in dispute. Hibbard, Molesworth, and others commenting on country-house poems accept the view of Tawney, Stone, and others that throughout the sixteenth and early seventeenth centuries the common people of England were victimized by rising rents and land enclosures.[2] The older aristocracy, whose expenditures (largely for dress and building) had become "modern," could not, during a century of terrific inflation, make ends meet with the traditionally fixed rents from their tenants. Their options were to enclose lands for pasturage, to raise rents or not grant new leases, and to cut expenses; housekeeping may have been the easiest to cut. In the meantime, a new class of city and country gentry, for whom land was a marketable commodity and not an inalienable basis of subsistence, were doing well. Treating their lands as private possessions or salable goods, they also, it is stated or implied, treated their tenants in the same way.

2 R. H. Tawney, "The Rise of the Gentry, 1558–1640,"*Economic History Review,* XI (1941), 1–38; Lawrence Stone, "The Anatomy of the Elizabethan Aristocracy," *EHR,* XVIII (1948), 1–53; Lawrence Stone, "The Elizabethan Aristocracy: A Restatement," *EHR,* 2nd Ser., IV (1952), 302–21; Lawrence Stone, *The Crisis of the Aristocracy, 1558–1641* (Oxford, 1965); L. C. Knights, *Drama and Society in the Age of Jonson,* 4th ed. (London, 1962).

Such an interpretation would be more convincing if the estate poems mentioned enclosures; but none does, although the practice was frequently attacked in Jonson's time. More disturbing is the ease with which Juvenal's Fifth Satire could be said to illustrate the same social and economic situation—one that it is perhaps both unfair and unwise to expect to see analyzed, or even accurately reflected, in a short poem. Moreover, the very existence of the conditions that Jonson is said to deplore is called into question by Hugh Trevor-Roper and W. K. Jordan.[3] Their analyses may of course be correct without altering the possibility that Jonson writes in misguided anticipation of Tawney and Stone, yet they may very likely persuade us to discount economic history as a tool in the analysis of estate poems. In answer to the usual charge (which was made during the sixteenth and seventeenth centuries as well) that the great system of ecclesiastical poor relief had been destroyed by the Reformation, Jordan argues that the Church charities had withered away during the fifteenth century, "yet we tend to yield to an illusion of the increase of poverty in England for a full century after our period begins [the sixteenth century], chiefly because men of the age were preoccupied with the problem, were earnestly engaged in trying to deal with it, and were for the first time coming to possess some knowledge of the facts" (*Philanthropy,* pp. 56–57).

Jordan sets 1485 as the terminal date for the historical forces of depopulation and deepening poverty, although,

3 W. K. Jordan, *The Charities of Rural England, 1480–1660* (New York, 1961); W. K. Jordan, *Philanthropy in England, 1480–1660* (London, 1959); Hugh Trevor-Roper, *Historical Essays* (New York, 1966); Hugh Trevor-Roper, *The Crisis of the Seventeenth Century* (New York and Evanston, 1968); Hugh Trevor-Roper, "The Elizabethan Aristocracy: An Anatomy Anatomized," *EHR,* 2nd Ser., III (1951), 279–98.

as he notes, the sixteenth century is the great age of "fierce and accusatory literature" on the subject (*Philanthropy*, p. 57). Trevor-Roper supports him in playing down the issue of land enclosures, which were, he argues, neither an important cause of poverty nor particularly prevalent after the early sixteenth century. On the other hand, a population growth of 40 percent during the sixteenth century and a further 30 percent between 1600 and 1640 explains the agricultural labor surplus.

Both Jordan and Trevor-Roper speak of the Tudor and Stuart regimes as "the great age of English charity," noting with impressive statistics that money flowed from the great London merchants into the countryside for the foundation and support of hospitals, grammar schools, and poor relief. It should be noted that if the poor had relatively little reason to complain, thanks were due to the generosity of London and Bristol merchants, who furnished 63 percent of the charitable wealth of the years 1480–1640 (*Philanthropy*, p. 241) and not to the landed nobility (*Philanthropy*, pp. 331–32), who had far less free capital. The latter fact may to some extent resolve the problem. Although Jonson's period was possibly not an impoverished one for anybody, the *traditional* sources of charity had dried up. The country-house poets do not acknowledge the good works of generations of city merchants, who found their historian in Fuller, author of the *Worthies*. Trevor-Roper concludes from Fuller's evidence that the age of Elizabeth and James, "so far from being an age of selfish individualism and spoliation, was the great age of collectivism, of social construction, of education and charitable endowment" ("Fuller's *Worthies*", *Historical Essays*, p. 128).

If Jonson indeed wished to argue the case of an indigent or dispossessed class, then the three lines in "To

Penshurst" that refer to victimized farmers are curiously negative and indirect:

> And though thy walls be of the countrey stone,
> They'are rear'd with no mans ruine, no man's groan;
> There's none, that dwell about them, wish them downe . . .

Throughout "To Penshurst" and the entire genre, in fact, the focus is never upon those who suffer on bad estates, but upon those who enjoy the liberality of good ones. Their security and happiness are stressed at the expense of the reputation of those who deny hospitality; but it is arguable whether such a juxtaposition suggests a "trend" towards a new order of society, or an ahistorical evaluation of the kinds of behavior that are either fruitful and to be encouraged or selfish and to be condemned. The penalty for the denial of hospitality—the limited form of charity that is the estate poets' subject—falls upon those denying rather than those denied. If Jonson recognized the supposed effects of capitalistic land policies, he is silent about the causes, preferring a moral and individual to an economic diagnosis of the disease. Thus, while Tawney and Stone may help us to understand what a seventeenth-century landowner was up against, they can tell us very little about how Jonson understood those problems, nor will we profit from translating Jonson's dichotomies into theirs.

The Contemporary Idealization of England

If we keep in mind the perspective of this research, we can evaluate more easily the overwhelming testimony of sixteenth- and seventeenth-century writers that the social contract was out of joint. In explaining the importance of ancient manorial customs to writers like Jonson, one must take notice of the English idealization of their country during the Renaissance, and the identification of national virtue with certain characteristics of country life. It is against this standard, implicit or not, that the new corruption is measured.

It was commonplace to think of England as the most favored of lands. Camden, who gently debunks many old stories, cannot resist reprinting a Roman panegyric of Britain as the fairest of all countries;[4] Procopius in his fifth-century *Gothic War* describes a delightful England, bordered by dreadful countries which we take to be Scotland, Wales, and Ireland.[5] A Renaissance dictionary describes the *Atlanticae Insulae,* or Fortunate or Blessed Isles, where the Golden Age survives (at least climatically and agriculturally),[6] and Camden explains that when Clement VI assigned the Fortunate Isles (the Canaries) to Spain, the British were convinced that he meant their countries (*Britannia,* I, li). History had made Britain the legatee of Troy (via the colonizing Brute), and her recent past, if we accept Shakespeare's well-known passages from *Richard II* and *Henry V,* only confirmed the special and glorious status that Heywood assigned her in *Troia Britannica* (1609). The Queen herself was frequently identified with Astraea, and it was believed by some at

4 *Britannia* (1586); ed. Richard Gough, 2nd ed. (London, 1806), I, 1.
5 Quoted in Edward Gibbon, *The History of the Decline and Fall of the Roman Empire,* ed. H. H. Milman (Paris, 1840), IV, 339–40.
6 The *Dictionarium* of Charles Stephanus, cited in DeWitt T. Starnes and E. W. Talbert, *Classical Myth and Legend in Renaissance Dictionaries* (Chapel Hill, N. C., 1955), p. 310.

least that her royal authority derived from that of Constantine, who also held supreme power over state and church; and that because the Tudors were of Welsh, or "ancient British" lineage, she had restored the line of Brute to the throne.[7]

Drayton in *Poly-Olbion* (1613; 1622) and Browne in *Britannia's Pastorals* (1613; 1616) mythologize the British and, more locally, Devon landscapes, which, though they seem to be Arcadias outside of time and history, have the flora and creatures of the actual island. Giles Fletcher's Britain, similarly, is ideally set apart from other countries because of its religion, an object of awe and envy to Europe. In England "the trustie earth sure plentie brings," as in the Golden Age (*Christ's Triumph After Death* [1610], stanzas 31, 33). Another aspect of the pastoral or near-pastoral idealization of the English countryside is the literary picture of games, sports, and such paraphernalia as maypoles. In the *Shepheardes Calendar* (the May eclogue), such pastimes are dismissed as Catholic and idle; but by the 1620s, at least, they have come to represent a timeless Merry England of innocence and unspoiled countryside.

Drayton, who complained to William Browne that

This Isle is a meere Bedlam, and therein,
We all lye raving,[8]

cheered up when Robert Dover instituted annual games, or "assemblies," in the Cotswolds:

---

7 See Frances A. Yates, "Queen Elizabeth as Astraea," *Journal of the Warburg and Courtauld Institutes*, X (1947), 27–82.

8 "To My Noble Friend Master William Browne, of the evill time" (undatable), *Works*, ed. J. William Hebel, III (Oxford, 1932), 209.

> Dover, to doe thee Right, who will not strive,
> That dost in these dull yron Times revive
> The golden Ages glories . . . [9]

Thomas Randolph, who wrote several poems in praise of country life, wrote an eclogue on the same assemblies and blamed the unsportive Puritans for the decay of games.[10] Ancient Greece and the recent past of England are vaguely yoked together as the "great good time," somewhat in the manner of Bishop Corbett, who idealizes the reign of Mary and sees a decline under Elizabeth. In "The Faeryes Farewell" (1647) he laments the decline of rural sports and criticizes Puritan severity.[11]

Jonson's *Sad Shepherd* (1637) is the best known work in this vein. His Robin plays host at feasts as well as at sports, and his England is perhaps the most successfully pastoralized of any. Palinode's argument in the May eclogue is here turned back upon him: it is "the sowrer sort of shepherds" who condemn the "rites" of music, song, and dancing; these are of course the Puritans, "hurried . . . with Covetise and Rage." This Arcadia of Sherwood Forest typifies an older civilization, now fading,

> . . . when on the Plaines,
> The Wood-men met the Damsells . . .
> Those charitable times had no mistrust,
> Shepherds knew how to love, and not to lust.
> (H & S, VII, 15–16)

9 "To My Noble Friend Mr. Robert Dover, on his brave Annuall Assemblies upon Cotswold" [1636], ibid., I (Oxford, 1931), 506.

10 "An Eclogue on the noble Assemblies revived on Cotswold Hills by Master Robert Dover," *Poetical and Dramatic Works,* ed. William Hazlitt (London, 1875), II, 621–26.

11 *The Poems of Richard Corbett,* ed. J. A. W. Bennett and H. R. Trevor-Roper (Oxford, 1955), pp. 49–52.

The mythological figures in Penshurst Park will seem more appropriate in conjunction with Jonson's men in Lincoln green; as one critic notes, they achieve "a definite naturalizing of myth in the geography of Great Britain."[12] If Jonson's lamentations suggest nostalgia for a disappearing England, his Sherwood Forest is still that green country so central to English sentiment: "the sense of a lost world associated with one's own youth or with the unspoiled springtide of civilization, for the Englishman, had more associations with greenery than with gold . . . To join the band of merry men and to wear Lincoln green was to renew one's contact with nature."[13] Using "such wooll, / As from meere English Flocks his Muse can pull" Jonson states his ambition, to make "a Fleece, / To match, or those of Sicily, or Greece." Such conjunctions of the green English countryside and the golden world of innocent love and "rites" are something like the metaphor of "garden" so frequently applied to the nation. Sylvester, before 1600, tinkered with *La Semaine* to insert a paean to Albion, "the World's rich Garden, Earth's rare Paradise,"[14] although by Marvell's time it had become "the Garden of the World ere while."[15] The Civil War gave Marvell and others, like Mildmay Fane (who writes similarly Anglophilic lamentations), cause to regret; but the initial assumption, that England was Paradise, is more interesting than the loss of faith. It was simply a commonplace to consider England a quasi-Arcadian or hortulan paradise, and the literary

12 G. B. Johnston, *Ben Jonson: Poet* (New York, 1945), p. 39.

13 Harry Levin, *The Myth of the Golden Age in the Renaissance* (Bloomington, Indiana, 1969), pp. 85–86.

14 Joshua Sylvester, *The Complete Works,* ed. Alexander B. Grosart (Edinburgh, 1880), I, 152.

15 "Upon Appleton House," *The Poems and Letters of Andrew Marvell,* ed. H. M. Margoliouth et al., 3rd rev. ed. (Oxford, 1971), I, 72.

invectives against the city[16] only reaffirmed the axiom, still an English commonplace, that the countryside is the "real" England.

The Hospitable Ideal and the Documents of Complaint

Before fixing the crisis of disillusionment too neatly in the early seventeenth century, one ought to note that the literature of complaint in England is ancient. During Mary's reign (admired by Bishop Corbett), George Cavendish looked back longingly at the "golden world" under Henry VIII; yet that prince's chaplain, Thomas Starkey, wrote of the terrible evils, especially enclosures and depopulation, within the commonwealth. He recommends a country life: "man at the begynnyng lyvyd many yerys wyt out any such pollycy [city life]; at the wych tyme he lyved more vertusely, and more accordying to the dygnyte of hys nature, then he doth now in thys wych you cal polytyke ordur and cyvylyte. We see also now in our days thos men wych lyve out of cytes and townys, and have fewyst lawys to be governyd by, lyve bettur then other dow in theyr gudly cytes never so wel byllyd and inhabytyd . . ."[17]

16 In *A Forest of Varieties* (1645), p. 68, for example, Dudley North complains of "costly and ill lodging and dyet, enforced neatnesse, importunate visits, perpetuall cap, curtesie, and complements, ceremonious acquaintance, tedious and chargeable businesse, pastime to seeke, his wonted healthfull exercise, Ayre and command turn'd to a sedentary and servile observance, and a sootie Ayre, such as the thickest rined vegetables rather pine then live in . . ."

17 *A Dialogue Between Cardinal Pole and Thomas Lupset,* in *England in the Reign of King Henry the Eighth,* ed. J. M. Cowper, Early English Text Society, Extra Ser., XII (London, 1871), p. 9.

The best qualities of English country life were found
in the manors, whose halls received and sheltered their
tenants, and whose tables sustained and cheered them. Or
so, by the time of Elizabeth, it is supposed to have been.
Chaucer's Franklin is perhaps a representative type:

> His table dormant in his halle alway
> Stood redy covered al the longe day.
> At sessiouns ther was he lord and sire.[18]

The Franklin followed the advice of a thirteenth-century
Bishop, Grosseteste, who said, "As much as ye may,
withoute peril of sykenes and weryneys, eate ye in the
halle afore youre meyne household for that schal to be
youre profyte and worschippe."[19]

Yet in Chaucer's time there were lords who preferred
to keep their distance, as William Langland complains:

> Elyng is the halle vche daye in the wyke,
> There the lorde ne the lady liketh nouȝte to sytte.
> Now hath vche riche a reule to eten by hym-selue
> In a pryue parloure for pore mennes sake,
> Or in a chambre with a chymneye and leue the
> chief halle
> That was made for meles men to eten inne;
> And al to spare to spille that spend shal an
> other.[20]

Perhaps one can detect in Grosseteste the complaint
made explicit in *Piers Plowman*; in any case, complaints of
this kind span several hundred years, finding without

18 General Prologue to *Canterbury Tales*, lines 353–55, in *The Works of
Chaucer*, ed. Fred N. Robinson, 2nd ed. (Boston, 1957), p. 20.

19 W. Shaw Sparrow, *The English House* (New York, 1909), p. 122.

20 *The Vision of William Concerning Piers the Plowman*, ed. W. W. Skeat
(Oxford, 1886), I, 292 (Text B, Passus X).

question their most polished, but also their final expression in "To Penshurst" and subsequent poems. Possibly Jonson writes at the end of a social revolution rather than at the beginning; in any case, the pamphlet literature of complaint in his time gives a distorted view of the changes in country life.

The documents are so many that a few must stand for the whole. "Servingmans Comfort," an anonymous tract of 1598, invests its glances backwards with the vision of the good old world:

> Now trueth it is, *in diebus illis,* in former ages, that Potentates and Gentlemen of worth spent their whole Rentes and Revenues in Hospitality and good Housekeeping . . . To compare . . . the pleasures of their golden dayes, when Gold was so smally regarded, with the miserie of this latter, nay last age, were able in my iudgement, to wring teares out of the eyes of Adamant. There was no violating of Fayth, no breach of promyse, no hatred nor mallice, no cunning nor Cunnie-catching, no swearing nor foreswearing, no fear of fraude, nor mistrust of friendshyp, no symonie, no briberie, no flatterie, no villany, no deceyte in bargaynyng, no false witnesse bearyng, no cruell murderyng, no craftie conspyring, nor any fraudulent dealing.

"And why?" we may well ask. "Because Golde, the authour of all this ungodlyness, was not regarded."[21] This

21 "A Health to the Gentlemanly Profession of Servingmen: Or, The Servingmans Comfort," in *Inedited Tracts,* ed. William Hazlitt (London, 1868), pp. 146–47.

commonplace picture of the Golden Age represents the old halls and manor houses of England; Gold, or Avarice, has destroyed hospitality.

One reason frequently cited for the decay of hospitality is the migration of gentlemen to London, in part perhaps because they could not keep up their establishments during an inflationary period while rents remained fixed. The pamphleteers do not dwell upon this financial squeeze, but attribute the decline of housekeeping to universal vices and to the ever unpopular enclosures. Phillip Stubbes, in the *Anatomy of Abuses* (1583) tells us that the English are very "inclyned to covetousness and ambition,"[22] and Robert Greene complains, in 1592, of

> the abuses that Pride had bred in Eng-
> lande . . . How since men placed their delights
> in proud looks and brave atyre, Hospitality was
> left off, Neighbourhood was exeiled, Conscience
> was skoft at, and charitie lay frozen in the streets:
> how upstart Gentlemen for the maintainance of
> that their fathers never lookt after, raised rents,
> rackte their tenants, and imposed greate fines.[23]

Greene also criticizes (if the word is not too mild) enclosures. The enclosure issue has been sufficiently called into question, however, by Trevor-Roper and Jordan—especially by Jordan's statistic (*Philanthropy*, p. 62) that only 1,200 square miles were enclosed between

22 Ed. Frederick J. Furnivall, New Shakspere Society, Ser. VI, No. 6 (London, 1877–79), pp. 114–15.

23 "A Quippe for an Upstart Courtier," *The Life and Complete Works in Prose and Verse of Robert Greene, M. A.,* ed. Alexander B. Grosart (London, 1881–83), XI, 209.

1455 and 1637—so that one is inclined to take Greene with a grain of salt.[24]

The same tendency to interpret the decay of house-keeping as both a universal and a national malady is apparent in a somewhat later document, Donald Lupton's *London and the Countrey Carbonadoed* of 1632. Pride is there, and covetousness, but "puritans" and "coaches" as well: "there are six upstart tricks come up in great Houses of late which he [hospitality] cannot brook Peeping windowes for the Ladies to view what doings there are in the Hall [an aperture of Penshurst dating from construction in 1347], a Buttery hatch that's kept lockt & cleane Tables, a French Cooke in the Kitching, a Porter that lockes the gates in dinner time, the decay of Blacke-iackes in the Cellar, and blew coates in the Hall." Clearly, the complaints have been brought up to date, but the sentiments are the same.

Lupton goes on to describe an ideal landlord but suggests that his kind is not to be found any more. His virtues were largely those of furnishing a table, but he knew how to be friendly: "Lusty able men well main-tayned were his delight, with whom he would be familiar: his Tenants knew when they saw him, for he kept the olde fashion, good, commendable, plaine: the poore about him wore him uppon their backes; but now since his death, Land-lords weare and wast their Tenants . . ."[25]

But a character writer of the year 1631 pictures "A Gentlemans House in the Countrey" in much the same

---

24 See also William Stafford, *Compendious or Briefe Examination of Certayn Ordinary Complaints . . . A. D. 1581,* ed. Frederick J. Furnivall, New Shakspere Society, Ser. VI, No. 3 (London, 1876), where country gentlemen are somewhat more sympathetically given the options of enclosing lands or decamping to London.

25 *London and the Countrey Carbonadoed and Quartered into Severall Characters* (London, 1632), pp. 100–01, 103.

agreeable way, with little suggestion (except by what is implicit in such idealizing) that such "housekeeping" has passed away.[26] Perhaps his is only the serenity of distance, for during the seventeenth century the old halls and manors came to be romanticized. John Selden writes, before 1654: "The Hall was the place where the great Lord us'd to eat (wherefore else were the Halls made so big?) Where he saw all his Servants and Tenants about him. He eat not in private, Except in time of sickness; when once he became a thing Coopt up, all his greatness was spoil'd. Nay the king himself used to eat in the Hall, and his Lords sate with him, and then he understood Men."[27] John Aubrey, in 1670, is equally captivated: "The Lords lived in their Countries like Petty Kings, had *Jura Regalia* belonging to their seigniories, had their Castles and Boroughs . . . The Lords of Manours kept good Houses in their Countries, did eat in their great *Gothick* Halls, at the High Table or Oriele, the Folk at the Side-Tables."[28]

What has happened, of course, is that the quasi-communal manorial society has become remote enough (existing still, as Aubrey notes, in Scotland) to become a subject of romance and to appear, in Selden's and Aubrey's descriptions, more like an invention of Scott than a Tudor or Jacobean household. Aubrey's use of the term Gothick puts us at a distance from the subject. John Evelyn, credited with popularizing the term, felt that in domestic buildings at least the abhorred style was no longer a threat. He writes in 1685 of an Elizabethan

26 Wye Saltonstall, *Picturae Loquentes* [1631, 1635] (Oxford, 1946).

27 *Table Talk*, ed. Edward Arber, English Reprints, No. 6 (London, 1895), p. 53.

28 *An Introduction to the Survey and Natural History of the North–Division of the County of Wiltshire* (London, 1720), p. 29.

manor, Swallowfield, that "the house is after the antient building of honourable gent: houses where they kept up the antient hospitality"; and of another, in 1700, "a noble old structure, capacious, & in forme of the buildings of the Age in Hen: 8. & Q. Eliz: & proper for the old English hospitality, but now decaying with the house it selfe . . ."[29] A less elegiac note is struck by a character in Shadwell's *Lancashire Witches* (1681): "For my part, I think 'twas never good days, but when great Tables were kept in large Halls, the Buttery-hatch always open, Black Jacks, and a good smell of Meat and March-Beer, with Dogs turds and mary-bones as Ornaments in the Hall: These were signs of good Housekeeping, I hate to see Italian fine Buildings with no Meat or Drink in 'em."[30]

By the eighteenth century, it is the Elizabethan age that assumes the mantle of primitive virtue. Dr. Arbuthnot, in Bishop Hurd's dialogue, contemplates the ruins of Kenilworth, and praises the entertainments and royal receptions in that castle as typifying a time when

> the arts of a refined and sequestered luxury were unknown . . . The same bell, that called the great man to his table, invited the neighbourhood all around, and proclaimed a holiday to the whole country. Who does not feel the decorum, and understand the benefits of this magnificence? The pre-eminence of rank and fortune was nobly sustained: the subordination of society preserved: and yet the envy, that is so apt to attend the great, happily avoided. Hence the weight and influence

29 *The Diary of John Evelyn,* ed. E. S. de Beer (Oxford, 1955), IV, 481; V, 427.

30 *The Complete Works of Thomas Shadwell,* ed. Montague Summers (London, 1927), IV, 136.

of the old nobility, who engaged the love, as well as commanded the veneration, of the people. In the mean time, rural industry flourished: private luxury was discouraged: and in both ways that frugal simplicity of life, our country's grace and ornament in those days, was preserved and promoted.[31]

Truly a remarkable verdict upon the Kenilworth of Elizabeth and Leicester!

The Ideal House

The pamphlet literature of the sixteenth and seventeenth centuries idealizes almost exclusively those aspects of manorial life that tend to bring master into close community with servants. Like Horace's waiters (Satire II, 6) or Licinianus' slaves (Martial, Epigram I, 49), the dependents of an ideal English manor are part of the family. These qualities of community and hospitality encourage the romantic backward looks of a later civilization. The country-house poems themselves take a larger view of old manorial values: to some extent they are anticipated by Sidney, who places the charitable virtues within a larger framework. In the *Arcadia* we find two houses whose design and functions are curiously contrasted. One is the house of Kalander, which could possibly have been based on Penshurst:

> Kalander knew that provision is the foundation of hospitalitie, and thrift the fewell of magnificence. The house it selfe was built of faire and

31 Richard Hurd, *Moral and Political Dialogues,* 6th ed. (London, 1788), I, 160–62.

strong stone, not affecting so much any extraor-
dinarie kinde of finenes, as an honorable representing of a firme statelines.

The opposition of "finenes" to the truly fine qualities of
"honor" and "statelines" is carried out by an architectural distinction: "faire and strong stone" is the stuff of
thrift and provision, thereby fundamental to the economy
that permits hospitality. The architectural descriptions
continue:

> . . . the lightes, doores and staires, rather
> directed to the use of the guest, then to the eye of
> the Artificer: and yet as the one cheefly heeded, so
> the other not neglected; each place handsome
> without curiositie, and homely without lothso-
> menes: not so daintie as not to be trode on, nor yet
> slubberd up with good felowshippe . . .

In a house utility is to be desired before beauty, the
two being opposed perhaps too arbitrarily as though one
were "being," the other "seeming": that is, however, the
basic assumption of country-house poetry. Sidney tries to
strike a middle ground and allow the eye some pleasures,
but I think these are not the pleasures of formal artistry.
They are rather pleasures induced by an appreciation of
the antiquity of the house, and of its society:

> all more lasting then beautifull, but that the
> consideration of the exceeding lastingnesse made
> the eye beleeve it was exceeding beautifull. The
> servants not so many in number, as cleanlie in
> apparell and serviceable in behaviour, testifying
> even in their countenaunces that their maister

tooke aswell care to be served, as of them that did serve.[32]

In the final clause Sidney hints at the mutual obligations of master and servants to fulfill their proper role. It is perhaps Basilius' conspicuous failure to fulfill his role, rather than any overt architectural condemnation, that makes the star-shaped lodge, Arcadia's other domestic structure, seem somewhat sinister. It is "of a yellow stone, built in the forme of a starre; having round about a garden framed into like points: and beyond the gardein ridings cut out, each aunswering the Angles of the Lodge . . ." Basilius' retreat, "not unfitte to flatter solitarinesse," is further landscaped in a manner that would appeal to Lancelot Brown. The hill on which the house is set "gives the eye lordship over a good large circuit, which, according to the nature of the country, being diversified betwene hills and dales, woods and playnes, one place more cleere, and the other more darksome, it seems a pleasant picture of nature, with lovely lightsomnes and artificall shadowes" (p. 91).

Sir Henry Wotton thought that the star lodge represented Basilius' escapism—he "did rather want some extraordinary Formes to entertaine his Fancy, then roome for Courtiers."[33] Although such a structure was by no means uncommon, a contrast between houses seems intended. Kalander might agree; he "spared not to remember how much Arcadia was changed since his youth: activitie & good felowship being nothing in the price it was then held in, but according to the nature of

---

32 *Arcadia,* ed. Albert Feuillerat (Cambridge, Eng., 1922), p. 15.
33 *Elements of Architecture* (1624); reproduction of the 1651 text in *Reliquiae Wottonianae* (Springfield, Mass., n.d.), p. 304.

the old growing world, still worse & worse" (p. 60). In the *Arcadia,* then, some thirty years before "Penshurst," we find what may be Penshurst itself memorialized as the type of the great English country house, possibly set in contrast to a modern structure remarkable for its conscious artifice, which itself may be a sign of degenerate times. The estate poems of a subsequent generation follow this model and corroborate the sentiments of middle- and lower-class pamphleteers. In Sidney's lovely description of the prospect from Basilius' house one can see also the idealization of nature, or simply topography, that is implicit in estate poetry. To the extent that the idealization of England is most fully realized in praise of the landscape and countryside, the estate poems, like the house of Kalander, are affirmations of a peculiarly English excellence. It is the sort of thing Victoria Sackville-West attributes to Knole, which she says

> stoops to nothing either pretentious or meretricious. There is here no flourish of architecture. It is, above all, an English house. It has the tone of England; it melts into the green of the garden turf, into the tawnier green of the park beyond, into the blue of the pale English sky; it settles down into its hollow amongst the cushioned tops of the trees; the brown-red of those roofs is the brown-red of the roofs of humble farms and pointed oast-houses, such as stain over a wide landscape of England the quilt-like pattern of the fields.[34]

34 *Knole and the Sackvilles* (New York, n.d.), p. 2.

The Verse Background

The estate poems of the seventeenth century are products of the revival both of Latin poets, especially Horace and Martial, and of such satiric and didactic Latin verse forms as the epigram and the verse-epistle. To a great extent, the revival of interest in Horace and Martial in the sixteenth century took the form of translations and imitations of poems in dispraise of court or city life, and in favor of rural retirement. If pastoral is the most important vehicle for such sentiments, nevertheless the Roman poem in praise of a simple life on the farm provided an appealing model for modern letters.

Surrey was the first in England to translate both Horace and Martial, choosing Horaces's Ode II, 10, "Praise of Mean and Constant Estate," and Martial's Epigram X, 47, "Vitam quae faciunt beatiorem." His concise rendition of Martial is a summary of many of the tangible and attainable virtues of country life:

> Martiall, the thinges that do attayn,
> The happy life, be these, I finde,
> The richesse left, not got with pain:
> The frutefull ground: the quiet mynde:
> The egall frend, no grudge, no strife:
> No charge of rule, nor governance:
> Without disease the healthful lyfe:
> The household of continuance:
> The meane diet, no delicate fare:
> Trew wisdom joyned with simpleness:
> The night discharged of all care,
> Where wine the wit may not oppresse:
> The faithful wife, without debate:
> Such slepes, as may begyle the night:

Contented with thine own estate,
Ne wish for death, ne fear his might.[35]

Like Horace's Second Epode, this epigram describes an abstraction of country life at no precise level of society. But it would seem to be a "household," and its timelessly good qualities are those which estate poets often particularize—for example, the faithful wife of the epigram resembles the chaste Lady Sidney of Penshurst. This epigram was popular; Kendall translated it for his *Flowers of Epigrammes* (1575), imitating Martial's "De Rusticatione," which specifically represents the activities of a large villa. Jonson's translation of X, 47, is more concise than Surrey's; Randolph's version amends "the richesse left" ("res non parta labore sed relicta") to the slightly more explicit "estate bequeath'd." Randolph also translates Claudian's "Old Man of Verona," which is in many ways like Martial's poem. Both Jonson and Randolph translated "Beatus ille . . . ."

These examples, picked from among many merely because they lie close to our estate poets and their sources, reveal the domestication in England of the antique ideal of farm life. A degree closer to the estate genre are poems that praise the beneficent qualities of retirement either on a particular English estate or for a certain person at a certain time. There is, surprisingly, a twelfth-century Latin poem by Marbod, Bishop of Rennes, which seems to anticipate the Renaissance praise of houses;[36] but

---

35 From T. K. Whipple, "Martial and the English Epigram from Sir Thomas Wyatt to Ben Johnson [sic]," *University of California Publications in Modern Philology*, X (1920–25), 317.

36 See J. P. Migne, ed., *Patrologiae Cursus Completus,* CLXXI (Paris, 1854), para. 1571. The introductory lines consititute a poem in praise of a country estate: Rus habet in silva patruus meus; huc mihi

closer to the mark are the concluding lines of Wyatt's satire, "Myne owne John Poynz." His praise of his seat in Kent (he specifies the location) is the pendant to a much lengthier complaint about the vices of court life, and it falls easily within the Latin tradition of such court / country oppositions. But Wyatt's is the life of an English gentlemen, not a philosopher, and he retires to Kent

> . . . to hounte and to hawke
> And in fowle weder at my booke to sitt.
> In frost and snowe then with my bowe to stawke,
> No man doeth marke where so I ride or goo.[37]

Two verse epistles that advance claims for the country are Barnabe Googe's "To Master Henry Cobham" and George Turbervile's "To his Friend Francis Th. leading his Life in the Countrie at his Desire." Court is contrasted with country, and hunting and hawking are admired. Similar activities are recommended years later, by Randolph in his "Ode to Master Anthony Stafford, to hasten him into the Country" and by Herrick in "A Country Life: To his Brother." In these two poems the life of the English countryside is identified with the Golden Age and with the past ("old simplicity," says Randolph); they are

---

saepe / Mos est abjectis curarum sordibus, et quae / Excruciant hominem, secedere ruris amoena; / Herba virens, et silva silens, et spiritus aurae / Lenis et festivus, et fons in gramine vivus / Defessam mentem recreant, et me mihi reddunt, / Et faciunt in me consistere; nam quis in urbe / Sollicita, et variis fervente tumultibus exstat, / Qui non extra se rapiatur, et expers / Ipse sui vanis impendat tempora rebus?

37 *Collected Poems,* ed. Kenneth Muir (Cambridge, Mass., 1963), p. 187.

indebted to Horace and Martial.[38] They are in no sense estate poems, but they refer us to the common store of sentiments about country life which estate poems presuppose. The estate poems of Martial, in much the same way, built upon the Stoical abstractions of poems like Epigram X, 47; and in England a parallel vision is developing.

Hall's Satire V, 2

Although Martial praises Faustinus' good relations with his tenants, and notes with approval that a friendly neighbor is asked to dine at the villa, there is little sense of the "open house" that English country-house poets seem to expect of the establishments they memorialize. Nothing in the Roman world, of course, resembles the ceremonious medieval dinner, and Faustinus' openhandedness, though important, is small beer compared to what was expected in England. It is possible that Jonson and his followers introduced the great manorial tables into their poems about country houses simply because they were obvious features of a well-run, though old-fashioned, establishment; it is also likely that they knew either the pamphlet literature of the age or the complainants themselves. But there is a source in poetry, which as far as I know has not been noticed.

Long before he had the ill fortune to tangle with Milton, Joseph Hall gained fame as—in his own mistaken words—the first English satirist, author of *Virgidemiae* (1597–98), "the gathering of rods." The satires follow

38 Randolph's poem is indebted to Martial, I, 55; Herrick's to Martial, IV, 29, VIII, 38, and X, 47, and to Juvenal, Sat. XI. See K. A. McEuen, *Classical Influence Upon the Tribe of Ben* (Cedar Rapids, Iowa, 1939), passim.

Juvenal, and Satire V, 2, is a loose adaptation of Juvenal's Fifth Satire, the story of the notorious banquet at Virro's. Hall's host, too, is called Virro, and he treats his guests in the same insulting fashion. The poem opens with a picture, not of Virro's house in town, but of a country house, perhaps one that Virro has left for the season. A wayfarer is approaching, but we are forewarned of inhospitality by the line "Hous-keping's dead." The house comes into view:

> Along thy way, thou canst not but descry,
> Faire glittering Hals to tempt the hopefull eye.

But alas,

> For never Syren tempts the pleased eares,
> As these the eye of fainting passengers;
> All is not so that seemes . . .

The familiar distinction of "being" against "seeming" is made, and the "seeming" has architectural specificity:

> There findest thou some stately Dorick frame
> Or neate Ionicke worke;
> Like the vaine bubble of Iberian pride [the
> Escurial],
> That over-croweth all the world beside.[39]

The architectural orders are the accoutrements of the animating vice of Pride—Pride that is also exemplified, Hall tells us, in masters who close their houses and go to town to spend a fortune on fancy clothes. Hall must have sympathized with the author of "Servingmans Comfort."

---

39 *The Collected Poems of Joseph Hall, Bishop of Exeter and Norwich,* ed. A. Davenport (Liverpool, 1949), p. 49.

Apparently this bauble of a building is all closed up, and the hungry traveler finds no relief at these "gay gates" and "proud piles." Among country-house poets, only Pope (if he be included) makes direct use of Hall's verses on the desolation of the great mansion, using them in his picture of the house of Cotta. Otherwise the "proud piles" criticized by Jonson and others have shadowy histories; it is usually assumed that their doors are open, but only to the few. Hall's hopeful wayfarer is directed to

> Beat the broad gates, a goodly hollow sound
> With doubled Ecchoes doth againe rebound,
> But not a Dog doth barke to welcome thee,
> Nor churlish Porter canst thou chafing see.

We see "the marble pavement hid with desart weede," and the smokeless chimneys.[40]

Hall's poem provides an important architectural model for Jonson. Although he describes no "good" old hall, he is explicit about the major failing of a "garish" (Hall's term) new one. And if his absolute separation of splendor or "seeming" from hospitality or "being" is just a commonplace, yet his details of the Roman orders on the façade of the house suggest that he has actual modern buildings in mind. There is evidence that Jonson knew Hall's satires—it would be surprising if he did not—and Satire V, 2, is the most obvious source of "those proud, ambitious heaps."

Perhaps a further reaching indebtedness is to the association of splendid architecture with the denial of

40 Barnabe Rich, in his *Farewell to the Military Profession* (ed. Thomas M. Cranfill [Austin, Texas, 1959], p. 15), compares his 1581 stay at Holdenby (Northamptonshire) with the lack of hospitality at houses "built with a great number of chimnies, and yet the smoke comes forth but at one onely tunnell."

specifically English modes of hospitality—for Bassus' villa, the Roman equivalent, was not linked to hospitality or to the absence of it, but to economics and utility. Martial merely praised Faustinus' good relations with his equals and his tenants, as Jonson would do in "To Penshurst"; but Hall, like the pamphleteers, insists upon the obligations of the manor towards the whole community of Christians—guests, tenants, and total strangers. Hall affirms this particularly English association of hospitality with charity, or love, implying at the same time that the manor house is (unlike a Roman villa) a central structure of society. These more serious obligations distinguish the manors of the country-house genre from their Italian originals.

3

The Architecture of the
Country-House Poets

The Traditional Manor and Its Plan

*T*HE ARCHITECTURE that is the object of praise
and criticism in the English country-house poems is
evaluated ethically, not esthetically. The distinctions
made between the routine of life on a good estate and a
bad one extend to an architectural dichotomy between
houses that are in various sentimental and demonstrable
ways built "naturally" and functionally, and houses the
design of which is unfriendly to traditional manorial
customs. The poets repeatedly lead us to a tableau of
communal feasting in the hall of the good old manor, and
the prestige of this apartment cannot be too strongly
emphasized. There the tenants and dependents of the
estate were, as Langland and Grosseteste suggested,
united with their betters for those meals so well represented in "To Sir Robert Wroth" and in Carew's poem on
Wrest. The decay of manorial hospitality may antedate
the decline of the hall in architectural importance, but
that decline was conspicuous in the architecture of
Jonson's day and might well suggest a correlation.

The solemnity of these important meals in the hall
depends on the juxtaposition of different classes of men, as

a description of meals given by Archbishop Matthew Parker at Lambeth Palace suggests:

> In the daily eating this was the custom. The Stewards, with the servants that were Gentlemen of the better rank, sat down at the tables in the Hall on the right hand; and the Almoner, with the Clergy and the other servants, sat on the other side; where there was plenty of all sorts of provision both for eating and drinking. The daily fragments thereof did suffice to fill the bellies of a great number of poor hungry people that waited at the gate; and so constant and unfailing was this provision at my Lord's table, that whosoever came in either at dinner or supper, being not above the degree of a Knight, might here be entertained worthy of his quality, either at the Steward's or at the Almoner's table.
>
> And moreover, it was the Archbishop's command to his servants that all strangers should be received and treated with all manner of civility and respect, and that places at the table should be assigned them according to their dignity and quality.[1]

It is to be expected, of course, that the distinctions of rank would be carefully observed, and just as the hall was built to accommodate such a large gathering, so did the layout of the hall include areas of high, middling, and low prestige. A description of a dinner given by Parker in 1570 suggests at least one reason for admitting the poor, and seating them at the lower end, while the important guests joined the hosts on the dais:

1 John Nichols, *The Progresses and Public Processions of Queen Elizabeth* (London, 1823), I, 203, n.

1. Penshurst: the south front,
showing Poulteney's original
building to the right of center.

At the remotest Tables, but in the same Hall,
in sight, sat the Poor of both Sexes . . . That by
looking on them, while they were Feasting, these
Archbishops and Bishops might in their present
height remember the merciful God that had
wrought great deliverances for them, and had
brought them to that State, out of their former
Dangers and Calamities; when they themselves
were poor and distressed: As the pious Archbishop meant, by so placing them.[2]

2 John Strype, *The Life and Acts of Matthew Parker* (London, 1711), pp.
303–4.

Hospitality of this kind was expected from important laymen, as well, at such times as funerals.

The earlier medieval manor was little more than the hall itself, and although private apartments appear as early as the twelfth century, the hall continued to outweigh them in both practical and architectural importance until about the beginning of the sixteenth century.[3] Penshurst Place and Haddon Hall (Derbyshire) preserve fourteenth-century halls in very nearly their

3 Nikolaus Pevsner, in *The Planning of the Elizabethan Country House* (London, 1960), p. 3, mentions Oakham (Rutland), of ca. 1185, as the first medieval interior with a fully developed layout of hall, service wing, and private apartments, or "solar."

2. Penshurst: the hall, looking
towards the screens passage
and the doors to the kitchen wing.

original condition. The open central hearth at Penshurst is typical of the period before walled fireplaces, a fifteenth-century innovation, were introduced, and the magnificent ceiling was made high to let the smoke dissipate. The plan of Haddon Hall reveals the growth of a medieval manor over several centuries as it extended itself segmentally from the hall. The manor of Haddon actually replaced an earlier church and walled enclosure on the same site, evidence of which is seen in the plan. The new structure consisted of three unequal elements common to most country houses of the period: the hall, the storage area to one end of it with the private "solar" or great chamber above it, and the service wing—pantry, buttery, and kitchen—at the other end. One enters the hall from the lower end (towards the service wing) by means of a passage separated from the main area of the hall by movable screens.

By Jonson's time, houses like Penshurst and Haddon, if they had escaped destruction or total renovation, had arrived at very much the state in which they appear today. If by comparison with the relatively small unit that made up the fourteenth-century houses they now seem enormous, still, their growth, as the complex façades and asymmetrical ground plans suggest, was never the product of a single builder guided by a consistent architectural vision, but rather of anonymous masons building ad hoc to suit the needs and tastes of the family as it grew. The effect of the façades of Penshurst Place is that of a pleasing harmony of asymmetrical and unmatched parts, developing there, as at Haddon, in roughly two directions: as wings were extended from the more prestigious end of the manor, the solar, to form ultimately an inner court, so were service apartments added from the kitchen wing to

finally enclose a lower, or base, court. Haddon Hall viewed from a distance conforms closely to the heath dun from which it takes its name, and in its relationship to the ground as well as in its freedom from applied ornamentation it suggests what was "natural" to Jonson's eye. Façades like those at Penshurst—strikingly harmonious resolutions of assorted masses and advancing and receding planes—sustain, in fact, a biological metaphor: the houses *grew,* adding apartments with little effort at axial symmetry and none at external stylization.

Spenser's Castle of Temperance, an important literary building, is quite faithful to the layout of Penshurst or Haddon. On a dais at one end of the hall sits a red-clad steward, and through it walks

3. Penshurst: from the northwest, showing fifteenth-
century additions at right
and Elizabethan construction
at the northwest corner.

A iolly yeoman, Marshall of the same . . .
. . . he did bestow
Both guestes and meate, when ever in they came,
And knew them how to order without blame,
As him the Steward bad.

(*Faerie Queene,* II, ix, 28)

Alma then leads her important visitors into the medieval
vaulted kitchen, placed, it would certainly seem from the
text, beyond one end of the hall, as it ought to be.

Thence backe againe faire Alma led them right
And soon into a goodly parlour brought,
That was with royall arras richly dight . . .

(II, ix, 33)

I do not think I am stretching a point to say that her course clearly lies "backe" through the hall to the private apartments on the other side. The synthesis of late-medieval domestic interior planning with the allegory of the human body is remarkable. It would belabor Spenser to overstress it, but the congruence reveals two notions, one consciously developed and the other merely implicit in the picture, of what is "natural"; the hall and its flanking apartments were thought to be just that.

4. Haddon: the west front.

During the quarter-millenium between the construction of Penshurst and Jonson's visits there, it acquired the absoluteness of a structure that is a part of nature, anonymously executed by masons unconfined by canons of style. To praise it is to praise nature; and its rival, the house or houses built to envious show, manifests its vices not in bad, or vulgar, architecture, but in architecture itself—which to Jonson can only have meant the Continental Renaissance as it was understood in England at the time. If by architecture we mean the conscious organiza-

55

tion of masses and stylization of façade, then it is architecture—buildings to which one must respond at first, and perhaps primarily, as works of art—that threatens Penshurst Place. Just how strange such a house would have seemed to men of the later sixteenth century can only be guessed as we compare the façade of Sir John

5. Haddon: the lower court,
with the hall in center.

Thynne's Longleat (Wiltshire), built over many years of
Elizabeth's reign, with an old manor: "architecture" in its
most formal sense has arrived. Three fronts of symmetrical square bays are united by an elegantly articulated
rhythm of multi-paned windows surmounted by a crisp
balustrade. As a piece of sculpture, a shaped thing,

57

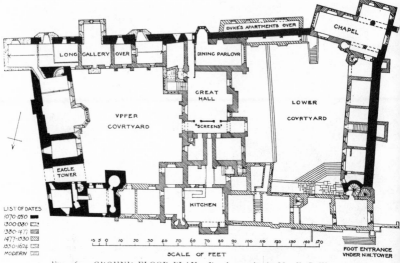

FIG. 161.—GROUND FLOOR PLAN.—Based on a plan by MR. E. G. WYLLIE.

6. Plan of Haddon Hall.

markedly horizontal and external (it stares at us), Longleat invites us to enjoy it as an object of art.

The stylistic origins of Longleat are obscure; nothing
like it is found again. But it is one of the first of the
"prodigy houses" of Elizabeth's and James's reigns, many
of which still defy classification in the history of European
building. That they are to some degree creatures of the
Continental Renaissance is probably true, but no Italian
would have recognized them as such. Until Inigo Jones
began building in the early seventeenth century, no
structure rose in England faithful to the Renaissance
architectural principles of symmetrical ground plans and
façades, strong horizontal lines and externality, and a
compact central block. (Longleat conforms more closely
than most.) The lavish application of the classical orders

7. Haddon: the hall, looking
towards the screens passage.
The woodwork on the screens
and the stonework tracery
around the windows indicate
the limits of ornamentation
in a manor of the thirteenth
or fourteenth century.

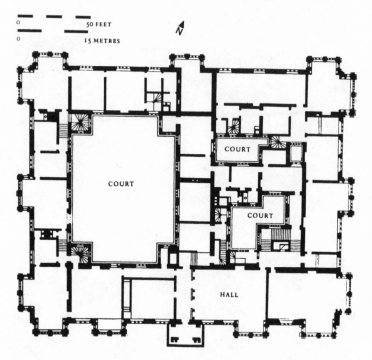

8. Longleat: plan of the
main floor, after the original
at Hatfield.

can be explained by the dissemination of Flemish and
German architectural textbooks, in which the originals of
the highly fanciful stonework of Wollaton Hall and other
houses are found. But the most important characteristic
of Longleat and the other new country houses is not their
loose adherence to Italian norms of architecture, but their
vast size and opulence, to which their formal elements of
plan, massing and façade are—at least for the poets—subsidiary. The prodigious new buildings were the work of
some rather prodigious men, political chiefs like Burghley

and industrial capitalists like Sir Francis Willoughby. The great wealth that made possible such luxurious detail of stone as one sees on the façade of Burghley (1556–87), or of wood on the hall screen at Longleat, must have encouraged the country-house poets to associate, even as cause and effect, "architecture" and extravagant display.

Their critiques suggest that the hall has been demoted, as a look at the plan of Longleat demonstrates. Unable to find any position of central importance within the gorgeous corset of the exterior walls, the hall lies uncomfortably along one side, indistinguishable from outdoors as a separate apartment. Although most Elizabethan and Jacobean halls grow in splendor, their structural singularity is at first muffled and at last cancelled out altogether. At Longleat, as at many later houses, the hall supports an upper story; at Burghley, despite its size, it sits uncomfortably to one side of an otherwise coherent and unified façade, and is approached from within as only one of a series of apartments *en suite*. It is difficult to say exactly when the family retreated to the private dining room (to which, in the sixteenth century, the old storage room under the solar was often converted), but the hall at Longleat was probably used mainly by the servants; and later houses pay rather perfunctory homage to what had been the room of greatest prestige.

We may say, then, that the houses built to envious show are guilty of sacrificing "natural" to "architectural" planning, and consequently of subordinating the position of the hall to the requirements of symmetry. They are guilty as well of conspicuous ostentation, for which the Italian Renaissance, filtered through mannerist textbooks only slightly understood, provided a dim authorization. The modern houses to which the poets refer fall roughly into two groups. In the work of Robert Smythson, and in

61

what have been called the "symbolic" houses of the late sixteenth century, a radical degree of stylization calls attention to the first uniquely English domestic *architecture*. In the country houses of the Cecil family and others, however, gigantism supervenes as the governing principle of building, and the medieval layout of apartments, easily recognizable despite distortions in most of the prodigy houses, reaches its last, elephantine stage. Both categories of houses are to some degree luxurious and splendid, and Jonson, demonstrably familiar with the second, probably knew the first as well. They are visible evidence of the pride and ambition he deplores in "To Penshurst."

Wollaton Hall, Nottinghamshire (1588), creation of the coal magnate Sir Francis Willoughby, is an important work of the architect Robert Smythson. Its most sensational innovation is the gigantic central story that rises

9. Longleat.

from the middle of the house. It is called a "lantern" because it derives remotely from a small aperture so called, located above the screens passage of a medieval house. A real lantern is in no sense a room. Nor was this immense apartment, lacking fireplaces and accessible only by a small staircase, intended as anything but an ornament; it must be the "lanthern whereof tales are told" in "To Penshurst." Framed by the ornamental stonework are gigantic windows that dazzle the outsider, approaching Wollaton from the base of a steep hill. It would be difficult to discover an element of architecture more naively designed to excite envy. Beneath the lantern, placed in the middle of the symmetrical house, the hall, retaining its screens passage, is inconveniently approached from the entrance way. The traditional service apartments are fitted in as best they can be.

10. Longleat: the hall, looking
towards the screens passage.

Sir John Summerson speaks of the conspicuous grandeur of Wollaton as symbolic, the objectification "of some symbolic or genealogical or merely geometric idea."[4] Both the functionless lantern and the vulgar, lavish, façade stonework that gives the weary eye no rest objectify Willoughby's wealth, and to Jonson they must have objectified "architecture" as an art of illusion and display.

But of all the curious directions taken by English houses of the period none is more bizarre, nor more symbolic in Summerson's sense, than the considerable body of houses, either executed or in plans and drawings, that represent immaterial ideas or embody ideal geometric relationships. Sidney did not have to resort altogether to his imagination to invent Basilius' star-shaped lodge, and in the drawings of John Thorpe and the buildings of Sir Thomas Tresham one sees much the same thing.[5] Tresham's triangular warrener's lodge, on the grounds of his Northamptonshire estate, is

> a trinitarian symbol of great complexity. The plan is a triangle and each of the three sides is surmounted by three triangular gables, while from the roof emerges a triangular chimney-shaft. All the windows are trefoils or built up of trefoils; the doorhead is a trefoil and an inscription announces the theme of the whole in the words *tres testimonium dant.*
>
> (*Architecture in Britain,* p. 79)

4 *Architecture in Britain, 1530–1830,* Pelican History of Art, 1st paperback ed. (London, 1970), p. 77.

5 R. H. Tawney mentions Sir Thomas Tresham as "the most hated encloser in his much disturbed county," an example of the "agricultural capitalists" of the seventeenth century ("The Rise of the Gentry, 1558–1640," *EHR,* XI [1941], 1–38).

Nor were such experiments confined to small or unimportant kinds of structures. Thorpe's design for a house in the shape of his initials was never realized, but Tresham nearly completed a manor in the form of a Greek cross, encircled with Latin salutations to Mary and decorated with roundels containing instruments of the Passion. Here, at Lyveden New Bield (Northampton-shire), function is subordinated to form in a complex way: while kitchens and service offices are banished to the basement, the body of the house is informed by the literary texts that dictate its religious symbolism, refer-ring us to a private and spiritual reality altogether outside

11. Burghley House: the hall
in foreground.

of architecture. It is easy to complain that Jonson simply
lacked the imagination to appreciate the energy of
English architecture of his time, but experiments like
Wollaton and the symbolic houses fall in the category of
toys, to which he compares the plastic arts:

What petty things they are, wee wonder at? like
children, that esteeme every trifle . . . they are
pleas'd with Cockleshels, Whistles, Hobby-horses,
and such-like: wee with Statues, Marble Pillars,
Pictures, guilded Roofes, where under-neath is

12. Wollaton Hall, 1580–88.

Lath, and Lyme; perhaps Lome. Yet wee take
pleasure in the lye, and are glad, wee can cosen
our selves. Nor is it onely in our wals, and seelings;
but all that wee call happinesse, is meere painting, and guilt.
(H & S, VIII, 607)[6]

6 Jonson's position is in fact ambiguous. As Stephen Orgel argues in
Inigo Jones: The Theatre of the Stuart Court (Berkeley, 1973), other
passages in *Discoveries* suggest a platonic admiration for image over
word or picture over gloss—despite his having taken a contrary
position in the quarrel with Jones.

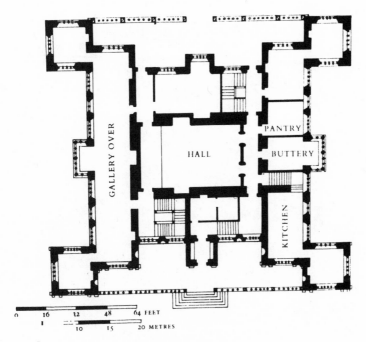

13. Wollaton: plan of the
main floor, after John
Thorpe's drawing.

Theobalds and Related Houses

The innovations in sixteenth-century domestic building were not altogether the work of "new men"—Willoughby and Tresham were already gentry of some standing; but the "new men," William Cecil, Sir Christopher Hatton, and somewhat later Cecil's sons, built the biggest homes. To the list of their houses—Cecil's Burghley and Theobalds (1564–85), Hatton's Holdenby (after

69

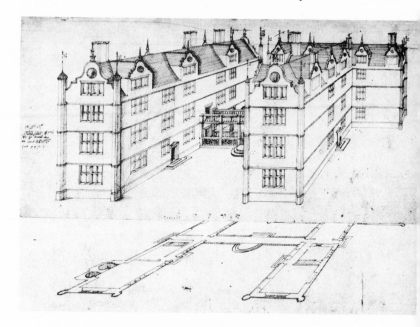

14. John Thorpe's design for
a house in the shape of his
initials, I. T.

1574), Thomas Cecil's Wimbledon (1588), and Robert
Cecil's Hatfield (1612)—must be added Audley End,
begun by Thomas Howard, Earl of Suffolk, in 1603 and
completed in 1616. They share a common hugeness and
magnificence with a certain conservatism in design
(Wimbledon possibly excepted), especially in the plan;
they were built by the leading statesmen of Elizabeth's
and James's reigns and, because of their quasi-public
functions, constitute the official architecture of the age.
Elizabeth built no palaces, although she encouraged her

15. Rushton: the triangular
warrener's lodge.

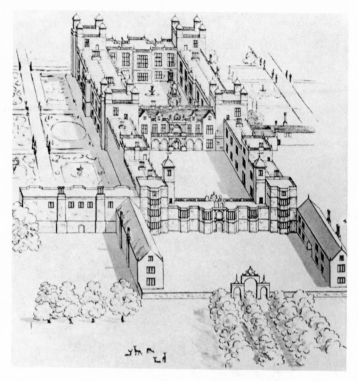

16. Theobalds: a reconstruction.

courtiers to build lavishly, and Theobalds, which received her on twelve progresses, became James's own house and the principal seat of government. Holdenby, the largest of the group, was bigger than Blenheim (excluding its flanking galleries) and with its gardens spread over 606 acres in a park of 1,789 acres.

It is unfortunate that Theobalds and Holdenby were destroyed under the Commonwealth regime, although the drawings and the estate map of Theobalds that survive from the seventeenth century give us a good idea

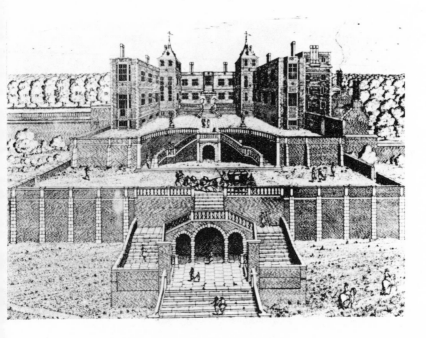

17. Wimbledon, begun 1588,
the Surrey estate of William
Cecil's eldest son, the first
Earl of Exeter (demolished
circa 1720). "A delicious
place for a prospect," wrote
John Evelyn.

of what it looked like. Audley End will suggest just as well
the gigantic and lavishly ornamented palace at which
Jonson probably received his Juvenalian snub from
Robert Cecil. At Theobalds and Audley End the traditional layout of a medieval manor has not been rejected,
but strongly asserted. At Theobalds, five courtyards
extend symmetrically along a quarter-mile axis, and the

73

ranges of building increase in height and are more densely massed as they recede along the axis. In this way, a complicated and dramatic movement of masses is achieved. At the rear, or "end," of the axis lies the Fountain Court, reserved for the Queen and her retinue; Cecil himself occupied rather modest quarters in the Middle Court.

What resulted is a splendid tableau, foreign to the spirit of a medieval house, yet essentially made up of medieval elements. Upon entering the principal gatehouse, one found the usual components of a great manor: a base court of service buildings flanked by two other courts, the Buttery and Dovehouse Courts, with equally

18. The ruins of Holdenby in the eighteenth century; the pair of arches at right survive.

> They come to see, and to be seene,
> And though they dance afore the Queene,
> Ther's none of these doth hope to come by
> Wealth, to build another *Holmby:*
> —Jonson, *The Entertainment of Althrope* (1603)

workaday functions. A yet more impressive gatehouse tower gave access to the Middle Court, which is roughly the equivalent of the inner court at, for example, Haddon Hall, except that the hall here is on the far side; the Fountain Court lies beyond it, reserved for the sovereign. As if by encyclopedic effort, Cecil has managed to pull every class of society, from the monarch to the artisan, into the confines of one house, delineating the status of each in the architecture of his building.

It is significant that the method of achieving splendor at Theobalds has little of the Italian Renaissance about it. Rather than building a compact central structure, looking outwards, Cecil depends upon a network of court-

yards that pull one inwards. Far from attempting to create a coherent series of façades, of roughly equal proportions on each side, he makes the house an experience of direct progress—from entrance to inner sancta, from large, open courtyards with low buildings to dense, smaller ones with lofty ranges all around. This is the random medieval plan trussed up and put on stage, and its purpose was doubtless to impress the great crowd of clients and office-seekers who never got far into the place, as well as the princes and imperial embassies who did.

19. Audley End, 1603–16: recession along an axis, with increasing height and greater density.

The hall at Theobalds was not small; it measured 60 by 30 feet and was decorated with artificial trees, fruits, and even birds' nests. But the hall was reduced to middling importance by the elaborate suites that surrounded it. It is likely that the Queen had little need of it, but it seems equally sure that the servants did not use it. The kitchens no longer adjoined the hall, but were situated in a court of their own. The servants were lodged in the corner towers—perhaps the earliest instance of their being domiciled in an attic, as they would be in the

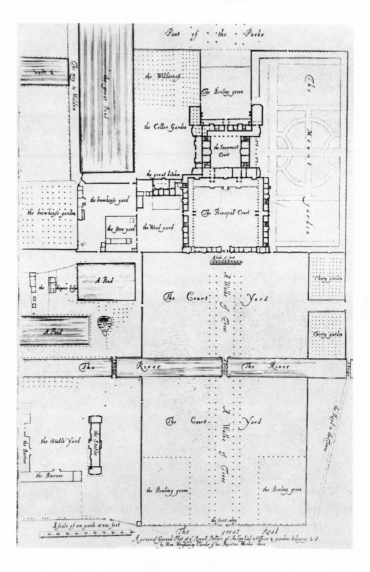

Part of the Parke

the Wildernesse

The Bouling green

the Celler Garden

The Somersett Court

the great kitchen

The Mount garden

the brewhouse yard

the brewhouse garden

the store yard

the Woed yard

The Principall Court

the way to Walden

the great End

A scale of feet

the Pompers lodge

A Pond

The Court Yard

A Walke of Trees

Chery garden

A Pond

Chery garden

The River

The River

The Court Yard

A Walke of Trees

the Stable Yard

the Stable

the Barnes

the Barnes

the Bouling green

A Walke of Trees

the Bouling green

the first entry

A scale of 100 yards or 200 feet

The great Road

A generall Ground Plat of ye Royall Pallace of Audley End & Offices & gardens belonging to it
by Hen Winstanley Clarke of his Majesties Workes there

20. Audley End: plan of the
estate, showing its Theo-
baldian derivation and the
organization of the buildings
and grounds along an axis.

eighteenth century. An internal network of communications—stairways and corridors—allowed the servants to go unobtrusively about their business, keeping them out of the hall (which would no longer be the principal passage between wings) and out of the guests' way as well. Theobalds is the first house, as far as I know, to isolate the staff so effectively from the "formal" areas of the house.

The contrast between Penshurst and Theobalds must have been striking. It is surely to be explained in part by the fact that Theobalds and the other houses built in imitation of it were avowedly designed to house the Queen in her progresses or, as Sir Christopher Hatton said of Holdenby, as a shrine to "that holy saint . . . to whom it is dedicated."[7] Such a house might seem a folly if one thought of it as a home, but Theobalds and Holdenby resemble Versailles more than they do Penshurst, and both were acquired by James I as royal palaces. Theobalds was, in 1607, the property of Robert Cecil, the earl of Salisbury and Jonson's host on the occasion of the serving of unequal fare. In that year he traded Theobalds to the King for the property of Hatfield (Hertfordshire), and sixteen other manors, and built the new Hatfield House on a modified Theobaldian pattern. It was completed in 1612, and there is evidence that Inigo Jones worked on it. Jonson must have been aware of the ongoing construction of the house, although it seems likely that Jones's contributions to the structure would have been architecturally less striking to him than the more obvious resemblance between Hatfield and its parent, Theobalds. At Hatfield the problem of entropic courtyards is solved by the consolidation of the house into a massive central block with wings, on an H-plan; the basecourt is located

to the rear of the building, and the humbler offices of the estate are invisible to one approaching the south entrance façade.

The Cecils' many houses, and Hatton's, were celebrated in their time for their splendor and luxury both of exterior ornament and of furnishings. The gardens were especially lavish; Thomas Fuller called those at Hatfield the "staple-place of earthly pleasure."[8] Intricately plastered ceilings; chimneys of colored marbles; entire rooms painted with the arms of families, the cities of Europe, the signs of the zodiac, the history of Rome, pyramids (in the hall at Holdenby)—all were noticed by foreign visitors and local historians alike. Tubbed orange trees, *jets d'eau,* and statues of the twelve Caesars dazzled the admiring guests.

8 *The History of the Worthies of England,* ed. A. P. Nuttall (London, 1840), II, 38.

21. Hatfield: the south
(former entrance) front of
1611, showing the H-plan
into which the house is
contracted.

Most conspicuous were the long galleries, one of the
few apartments in the English country house that is an
innovation of the sixteenth century. Long galleries are
rooms of conspicuous leisure and the best place for the
display of the luxury of glass, the emblem of fashion and
wealth in domestic building. Perhaps because the con-
traction of the medieval ground plan into a symmetrical
and increasingly centralized mass tended to force the
builder to reach skywards, long galleries are usually found
on upper stories, attaining at Hardwick Hall, Derbyshire
(a Smythson house) an extravagance of height and
splendor. Wimbledon had two galleries, one gorgeously
painted and marbled; that at Hardwick is furnished with
tapestries purchased from Hatton at the high cost of £325.
The dimensions of the galleries are as striking as the vogue
that made them de rigueur. In 1600 Sir John Manners
put up a 100-foot gallery overlooking the gardens of

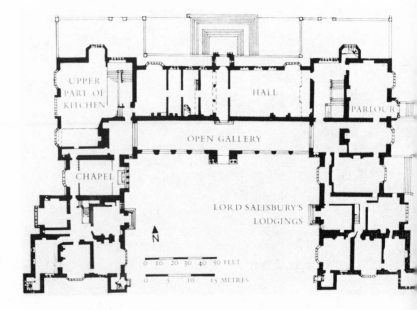

22. Hatfield; plan of the main floor;
the hall lies asymmetrically
to the left of the north entrance.

Haddon Hall, and at Audley the gallery measured 226 by
32 feet. Disproportionate apartments of this kind make
English architecture the despair of the mandarins of taste.

Bacon's Ideal House

Sir Nicholas Bacon, lord privy seal, had just built a
new house in 1568, but the Queen found it too small and
persuaded or bullied him to add a gallery of 120 by 18
feet. Perhaps it was the success of this room, panelled in
oak gilt and adorned with Latin inscriptions, that in-

23. Hardwick Hall: west
front from the garden.

duced Sir Nicholas' famous son to insist on "stately
galleries" in his essay "Of Building." Bacon's essay is in
every way the picture of the great Elizabethan palace-
house, like Theobalds or Burghley, and despite a spacious
emphasis on magnificent public rooms, it corresponds
exactly to the great houses he was used to. His criticism of
the curtain-wall of glass points out the purely spectacular
quality of what was new in Tudor and Stuart house
design. But in other respects, and despite the opening
sentence, "Houses are built to live in, not to look on;
therefore let use be preferred before uniformity, except

24. Haddon Hall: the Long
Gallery of circa 1600.

where both may be had," Bacon opts for magnificence.
He requires a public and a private sector for the house,
noting rather grandly that one needs "a side for the
banquet, as is spoken of in the book of Esther, and a side
for the household; the one for feasts and triumphs, and
the other for dwelling."[9]

In most respects the "palace" corresponds to Theobalds or Hatfield. A large central tower dominates the
façade; there is a great hall, and parlors; kitchens are in

9 "Of Building," *Bacon's Essays*, ed. Guy Montgomery (New York,
1940), p. 112.

the basement. The house has a large base court of low buildings (like Audley End), exterior staircases "cast into turrets," and an inner court behind the central structure with garden around and beyond it. In insisting on such minutiae as fountains and statues in the inner court, four bay windows over the basecourt, and a staircase garnished with "images of wood cast into a brass colour," Bacon seems excessively particular and probably has Theobalds on his mind. Like Theobalds, this palace has two unenclosed forecourts adjacent to the base court, the offices at a distance connected by "low galleries." Like every new house of the times, the building is externally symmetrical but internally somewhat random ("uniform without, though severally partitioned within"); and there is a peculiar reference to an "infirmary, if the prince or any special person should be sick," perhaps as a result of Jacobean licentiousness.

"Of Building" is not a very imaginative document. It is valuable because it sums up the ground plan and decor of the normative mansion of the time, which is Theobalds; and because it dilates with the obvious pleasure of stylishness upon such features as open loggias and second-story galleries, and little banqueting houses, "two delicate or rich cabinets, daintily paved, richly hanged, glazed with crystalline glass, and a rich cupola in the midst." All this is the *dernier cri* (he also asks for running water, though only in the gallery!), but the ground-plan is still close to that of Haddon Hall. The staff are mentioned only once: Bacon recommends that the servants' dining hall not be near the foot of the staircase because the odors of food "will come up as in a tunnel." This is perhaps an injunction against feeding servants in the hall, from which the master of the house has probably vanished. There is as yet no mention of a dining room.

At Theobalds, a network of passages enabled the servants to pass silently about the house, attending to their duties, and not be brought together in the hall or at any one spot. Bacon's central block preserves the antique tripartite structure; but with the kitchens in the basement and the "offices" at a distance, the hall is balanced by the great banquet area, which would serve for royal receptions or for private entertaining on a grand scale. This

25. Hardwick Hall: the
Long Gallery.

resembles the basic structure of Hatfield, where "the
family lived on the ground floor of the east wing, where
they are to-day, while the first floor of the east wing
contained the King's apartments and the west those of the
Queen, the two linked by the Long Gallery."[10] The
concept of entertaining, or "giving parties," is remote

10 Lawrence Stone, "The Building of Hatfield House," *Archaeologi-
cal Journal*, CXII (1956: for 1955), 101.

from a medieval household, where dinner could be said to have been a permanent "feast" (however spare in practice) open to all comers but not staged for their benefit. The entertainments contemplated by Bacon—or by noblemen receiving Elizabeth and James, or by James himself at Theobalds—are quite a different thing. The attention of the masters is diverted from the household (their inferiors) to the guests (their equals or betters). In the cautious manner so typical of the English planner, Bacon has adapted the hall and its balancing element into the "public" and "private" sectors, with feasting and such good times identified with important guests, not dependents and strangers.

Bacon's essay is not innovative on the subject of massing. A look at Audley End today, though it has been stripped of its forecourts, suggests that the multiplying courtyards of greater and greater dimensions make a house of endless ranges; the distances to traverse become enormous, just as the courtyards seem arbitrary and useless. Houses like Hatfield had got beyond the courtyard principle, a fact which indicates, again, that Bacon has Theobalds as his principal model.

The Private Home

For all its splendor, Hatfield is the house of a private man, not the palace of a sovereign. It suggests that the English country house of Jonson's time would develop ultimately, not into something like Versailles or Vaux-le-Vicomte, but into an intensely private retreat, one in which the supposed largesse of the medieval manor must be qualified by the terms of friendship or privilege existing between the master of the estate and those enjoying his hospitality. Thus it is not only at magnificent Theobalds that one may see the nemesis of the traditional manor, but also in houses where the desire to gratify either the builder's pride or his vanity or his sense of architectural beauty, or simply the desire for the luxury of a well-appointed private life, might override any vision of a new house as the spiritual and material center of a community of men.

If a manner of house-building that calls attention to itself, a manner of construction observing formal principles of elevation, massing, and ground-plan, be called "architecture" by contrast with the simple "building" of the fourteenth-century manor house, then the development of a distinct architectural idiom throughout the career of a single architect could be seen as the antithesis of the anonymous medieval style. Robert Smythson's Hardwick Hall (1590–97), a striking formal triumph, is antithetical both to Theobalds and to Penshurst. It exemplifies far better than Wollaton, Smythson's earlier work, that a house can be the product of a personal vision—in this case, that of Smythson and of Elizabeth, countess of Shrewsbury (Bess of Hardwick).

The great luxury of the house—its curtain-walls of glass, as well as the Long Gallery, are outstanding—ministers to an individual's obsession, for Bess was a prodigious builder. Not surprisingly, she made short shrift of the hall, where no dais can ever have existed, and in fact had it run across the center of the house rather than along the horizontal axis. The important rooms are high up, where the greatest advantage can be taken of the views afforded by the giant windows. Perhaps the real significance of Hardwick is the fact, so commonplace to us, that it was built by an experienced architect on a private commission, and bears little or no relationship to the

26. Montacute.

community around it. Such a change in the concept and construction of a country house suggests many metaphors and analogies: from community to the individual, from anonymous to idiosyncratic design, from utility to display, from timelessness to "modernity," and, stylistically, from horizontal to vertical thrust. Hardwick seems to be the self, writ large; it seems altogether fitting that Hobbes died there, in 1679.

At Montacute House, near Yeovil, the point made so fiercely at Hardwick is insinuated with gentle understatement. Built about 1599, it is said to be of all Elizabethan houses the most charming; that charm is owing in large degree to the house's unassertive richness. The rooms are conventionally laid out, with the hall dividing the important from the humbler apartments. But these rooms are domesticated. The hall has a simple flat ceiling and supports an upper story, and its screen is a piece of

furniture rather than a barrier. Externally symmetrical, the house could be the central part of a Theobalds or an Audley End, and one could expect ranges of buildings forming courtyards around it.

But those "lodgings," or courtyard buildings, have been lopped off, and while no lower or middle courts block access, neither do curtain-walls of glass strive to impress. What would have been the courtyard in front has become a garden, surrounded by a low balustrade that is punctuated by little turreted banqueting houses, and the border of herbs and flowers (laid out by Victoria Sackville-West) accentuates the delicacy of the stonework. Here the builder has indulged himself in the Elizabethan vogue of neomedieval fantasy, the sort of illusionism found in the paper castles assaulted at tournaments, and in the *Faerie Queene*. The architectural impression is well described as that of an old fortified manor house under a

91

covenant of grace: "The gatehouse has become a gateway, the curtain walls open balustrading, the bastions toy temples, the corner towers bower-like pavilions."[11]

Summary: The Tudor-Stuart Country House

The domestication of Gothic romanticism in the forecourt architecture of Montacute is one example of the luxurious, idiosyncratic, and purely decorative elements that by 1600 had become part of the English country house. The acceptance of the principle of conscious design and display in domestic architecture implies a change in the attitude towards country houses, and towards the country itself, rather like the difference between Constantin Levin's feelings and Koznyshev's in *Anna Karenin*. It is less surprising to find conspicuous splendor at Theobalds or Holdenby; those estates were tacitly royal palaces, and if Theobalds began as a manor, it ended as the rival to Greenwich and Hampton Court.

At Montacute or Hardwick, however, the official justification for splendor and luxury is absent; one finds instead an obvious desire to follow a style, to impress the neighbors, and to gratify the owner's desire for magnificence. Such sentiments had little place in an earlier England, and they must be explained in part as a product of the new "county society." Thus, in the fifteenth and early sixteenth centuries, we find the Pastons of Norfolk at actual war with their peers and neighbors, but allied "vertically" through a system of patronage and vassalage to greater and lesser families in Norfolk, London, and

11 H. Avray Tipping, *English Homes: Late Tudor and Early Stuart* (London, 1922), I, 204.

across the country.[12] By the close of Elizabeth's reign something like the modern system of "horizontal" class loyalties had developed. The big money was to be found in London, or in industries (like Willoughby's coal-mining), or on the sea. Although agriculture could scarcely lose its importance, it had ceased to be the universal source of wealth. Men who made their fortunes elsewhere returned to their villages and estates to build houses that would represent the fruits of their labors. They founded county society.

To the extent that the country came to represent leisure, country houses represented achievement; architecture gave outward form to success, and gratified the desire for conspicuous luxury. The generally conservative English were never eager, however, to break with the manorial traditions of an earlier age, and in the newest and most radical houses medieval apartments survive with tenacity. But the new function of the country house was better expressed in the expanded private apartments, and the hall, as at Hardwick, was probably abandoned to the servants. The trends that the seventeenth-century poets deplore are characteristics of an age when the country had come to represent, to the wealthy, both an escape from the city and a retreat into "the past." Even the poets feel this way, presenting life on estates like Penshurst or Wrest as a timelessly ancient cycle of harvest and hospitality. They deplore the pomp and vanity of the newer houses, without realizing that their own urbane tendency to pastoralize is not far distant from the state of mind of a Thynne or a Bess of Hardwick, who turned the fields and meadows into gardens and parks, and farms into fairies' castles.

12 See H. R. Trevor-Roper, "Up and Down in the Country: the Paston Letters," *Historical Essays* (New York, 1966), pp. 98–102.

The Architecture of the Country-House Poets

The prestige of Inigo Jones, the first Englishman to build with fidelity to the spirit of Italian Renaissance architecture, has led G. R. Hibbard to conclude that his work and that of his school constitutes the new architecture attacked by Jonson and others. The thesis is attractive, because Jones's work was radical in Jacobean and Caroline England, and because the neoclassical country house of the late seventeenth century does show that formal magnificence and remoteness from traditional manorial design which seem to characterize the wicked structures of the country-house genre. The difficulties of accepting Hibbard's argument are ones of dating, and of the exact style of building attacked in the poems.

If Jonson's poem was written no later than 1612, then Jones's hand in the "proud, ambitious heaps" rests on the slender body of his work completed before that date. The designs for stage architecture, however unpalatable to Jonson, are no threat to Penshurst Place. Jones's unexecuted designs for St. Paul's and Britain's Burse (1608) seem feeble candidates, as does Jones's first recorded architectural commission, a funeral monument in Shropshire (before 1610). Jones may have worked on Hatfield after 1608, but his contribution offers few clues to the kind of work that was to make his architectural reputation, and Jonson is an improbable candidate for the role of sybil in discerning them. Jones's position after 1608 was such that the Earl of Salisbury and the Prince of Wales looked to him for advice in architectural matters. In 1606 Edward Bolton had expressed the "hope," in a book inscribed to Jones, "that sculpture, modelling, and architecture, painting, acting and all that is praise-worthy in the elegant arts of the Ancients may one day find their way

27. Swakeleys (1638), the home of
a merchant who became
Lord Mayor of London.

across the Alps into our England."[13] But in 1612, Jones's
architectural accomplishments suggested no dominance
over the English landscape of things "built to envious
show."

If Jones's work after his Italian journey of 1613–14
influenced later country-house poems (up to Carew's on
Wrest, circa 1639, and Marvell's on Appleton House,
circa 1652), then one would hope to find a body of

13 Oliver Hill and John Cornforth, *English Country Houses: Caroline,
1625–85* (London, 1966), p. 12.

Caroline country houses in a fully realized Palladian style—one that constitutes a clear departure from the architecture of the medieval mason, as well as from that of the prodigy house builders. But Jones's work was for the most part executed in London, and with the possible exception of the Queen's House, Greenwich (1616–35), cannot have been expected to fulfill the purposes of rural manor estates. No country house has been named with certainty as Jones's own work, although Stoke Bruerne, Northamptonshire (1629–35), is a candidate. In the body of prewar country houses to which Jones or his pupils may

28. Blickling Hall (1616–27): a country house contemporary with Jones's Queen's House. The chimneys, gables, and ogee-capped towers, and the red brick, preserve the elements of Tudor ornamentation, with some Flemish overlay.

have contributed interior or façade architecture one cannot find a dominant, new, Italian movement in the act of displacing conventional modes of building.

Jones's influence was immense, but it was a delayed influence; it is difficult to believe that Herrick, Carew, or Marvell would have found the genesis of the neoclassical country house in the interiors and façade work at Houghton Conquest (1615–21), Raynham Hall (after 1619), Wilton (1633–40), Kirby (1638–39), Castle Ashby (of uncertain date), and a handful of other partially remodeled houses. In 1652, the probable date of the

composition of Marvell's poem, Sir Roger Pratt began building Coleshill (Berkshire). He had said on his return from Italy in 1649 that "architecture here has not received those advantages which it has in other parts, it continuing almost still as rude here as it was at the very first."[14] A cruel evaluation, surely, of the efforts of Thynne,

14 R. T. Gunther, *The Architecture of Sir Roger Pratt* (Oxford, 1928), p. 60.

29. Inigo Jones: the Queen's
House, Greenwich (1616–35).

Hatton, the Cecils, et alii; but one suggesting the scarcity
of what Pratt, a disciple of Jones, would call true
architecture. As the country-house genre came to a close,
the seeds planted by Jones finally were flowering into the
neoclassical country house of which Hibbard speaks.

The importance of Jones's influence upon prewar
country houses would have been only dimly perceived
amidst the much coarser novelties of the dominant

99

Caroline style, which was Flemish in inspiration but not unlike the late Elizabethan manor. If Audley End is the last of the giant prodigy houses, still, the ornamentation of Swakeleys, Middlesex (1629–38), preserves the elaborate exterior stonework of Hatfield and Wollaton. Carew's "Dorique" and "Corinthian" pillars are found in new houses of the twenties and thirties, like Balls Park (Hertfordshire): "the pilasters at the corners of the façade are flanked by inward and outward-looking quoins; Ionic capitals on the upper pilasters support carved consoles, while brackets are placed in pairs between the windows."[15] In short, the Caroline country house was likely to be a fussy, ornamented structure, alien to the spirit of Jones and Palladio yet the antithesis of the "natural" medieval house. The Hall survives at Swakeleys, in something like a traditional position, and there is little in the work of the artisan mannerists (the phrase is Sir John Summerson's) to suggest a sharp break with the recent past.

Hibbard states that the buildings of Jones and his school "began to affect the design of the large country house and after the Restoration became the dominant mode."[16] Although the statement is in a sense true, it does not bear upon the architecture attacked by Jonson, Herrick, and Carew, whose poems on houses date from about 1610 to 1639. "Appleton House" might have been written with an eye to a house like Wilton or Stoke Bruerne (Carew's poem on Wrest postdates these houses as well). But besides the fact that there is no evidence of

15 Hill & Cornforth, p. 22.
16 "The Country House Poem of the Seventeenth Century," *Journal of the Warburg and Courtauld Institutes*, XIX (1956), 159–74.

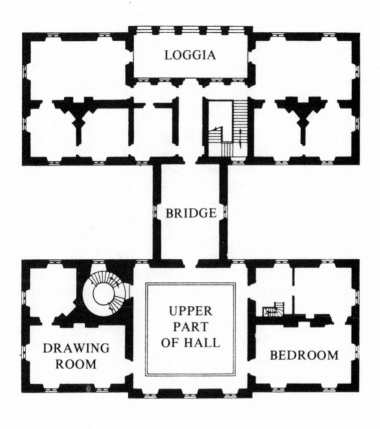

LOGGIA

BRIDGE

DRAWING ROOM

UPPER PART OF HALL

BEDROOM

30. The Queen's House: plan of the first floors of 1635. The hall of the Queen's House is a perfect cube.

Marvell's knowing either house, there is also no justification within the stylistic terms of his own or the other five
country-house poems.

The architecture attacked by Jonson is outstanding
both for size ("proud, ambitious heaps"), and for richness
of materials ("touch, or marble . . . polish'd pillars . . . roofe of gold"). Herrick imitates him ("marbles," and "Pillars . . . of lasting Jet"), and Carew adds
the more exotic touch of "Piramids, and high / Exalted
Turrets," and speaks also of rich materials ("a Pile
. . . / Of carved Marble, Touch, or Porpherie
. . . Dorique, [and] Corinthian Pillars"). With the exception of the orders, which demonstrably had been part
of the stonemasons' vernacular since the introduction of
German and Flemish texts under Elizabeth, nothing in
these descriptions could be further removed from the
chaste and modestly proportioned architecture of Inigo
Jones or, for that matter, of Palladio's villas.

Jonson had the model of Theobalds, where he was
once badly treated at the dinner table, and which
corresponds closely to the extravagant "envious show"
which he describes. The later poets of the genre work so
closely within his terminology that it is unlikely that they
had any new architectural ideas; but in any case, the
paucity of neoclassical domestic architecture before the
Restoration, and especially before 1652, should preclude
any association of the poets' complaints with the style of
Palladio. Pope, writing easily within the conventions of
the genre, criticizes what can be interpreted as a neoclassical manor for faults of the kind criticized decades
earlier. It is probably through a process of "reading
backward" from Pope's *Epistle to Burlington* and *Epistle to
Bathurst* that Hibbard established his medieval / neoclassical dichotomy.

Jonson had another quite attractive model for his wicked country establishment: it was literary, but it might also have been modeled on a house like Wollaton or Theobalds. And if Jonson mentions a house built to "envious show," he had a model with a deadlier flaw in its structure:

> A stately Pallace built of squared bricke,
> Which cunningly was without morter laid,
> Whose wals were high, but nothing strong, nor thick,
> And golden foile all over them displaid,
> That purest skye with brightnesse they dismaid:
> High lifted up were many loftie towres,
> And goodly galleries far over laid,
> Full of fair windowes, and delightfull bowres;
> And on the top a Diall told the timely howres.
> (*FQ*, I, iv, 4)

The House of Pride boasts very nearly one of the features that Penshurst, happily, does not have: the "roofe of gold." The reference to a gallery is also interesting, in view of its fashionable and leisurely connotations. The clock tower, a Flemish motif, is prominent at Burghley House; "loftie towres" are also familiar. Spenser may have had the castles of old romance in mind; but many of the Elizabethan prodigy houses antedate the 1590 publication of Books I–III of the *Faerie Queene,* and might easily have served as a model for Spenser and possibly through him to Jonson. If this is true, then the presence of Italian Renaissance architecture in the country-house poem is difficult to recognize.

4

Jonson, Carew, and Herrick

The Country Houses and Their Role:
Architecture and Grounds

THE ESTATES that Jonson, Carew, and Herrick
celebrate are valuable because they afford their owners a
living and render services to the community. This is not to
say that they are merely property, like the villas described
by Varro and Columella; in fact they are old, even
ancient, demesnes, where an economy of agricultural
production and a system of human relationships has
evolved independently of urban civilization. These
houses therefore are to be distinguished from retreats,
however grand or however (in the manner of Horace's
Sabine villa) functional, because they offer not an alternative to the city but a way of life that antedates the city.
The poems, other than "To Sir Robert Wroth," consider
the manors on manorial terms, and compare them not
with the town but with another sort of country house; the
poems therefore fall outside of the Horatian or *beatus ille*
tradition.

The virtues of these estates, similarly, are public and
somewhat diffuse rather than private and ideal. That is,
they are virtues of economics and human relationships
touching upon all the classes of society embraced within

the poems, from King James down to the tenants, and even to the animals and the fruits of the garden. We are not concerned here with repairing the damage done by the stress of city life, nor with the analysis or exposition of nature's redeeming qualities, but with the functioning of a particular system, the manor, located in the context of England and of history and recognized as a fundamental unit of the English body politic. The virtue of the estates is utility.

Utility, in these poems, takes the form of hospitality, an apparent contradiction that is resolved by the inclusion of charity (in the religious sense) within the economics of the house. There is a moral economy operative here: the functioning of the estate depends upon the observing of the proper relationships between the classes of society or between the offices of the estate. The lords, major-domos, guests, servants, tenants, and wayfaring strangers are brought together, at least in theory, in the great hall—which indeed was designed for the purpose and provides the central image with which these poets work. In the rendering of goods and homage to the master, and in the feeding and protecting of the household by the master, the poets find the most convenient image of the larger household economy that includes agriculture, tithes, paying of wages, and so on. All these estate activities are represented by the meal in the great hall; its importance is an indication of how much the medieval ties of lord to underling differ from those of the Romans. The generic emphasis upon these expansive reunions at table takes, of necessity, an archaizing position. If we are not to feel that this is merely a meal, we must have a picture that is somewhat abstract, emblematic, idealized; an important device is the link with the Golden Age, and with the deities of pastoral literature.

Thus Pan, and Sylvane, having had their rites,
    Comus puts in, for new delights;
And fills thy open hall with mirth, and cheere,
    As if in Saturnes raigne it were . . .
Such, and no other was that age, of old,
    Which boasts t'have had the head of gold.
(H&S, VIII, 98)

Herrick praises Sir Lewis Pemberton for entertaining "as the old Race of mankind did," saying

Thou do'st redeeme those times; and what was lost
    Of antient honesty, may boast
    It keeps a growth in thee . . .[1]

In these "open halls" with their "route of rurall folke" one finds the imprint of Astraea, as Vergil did with his rustics; at the same time the English past is fondly evoked. The prestige of the age of gold dignifies, explicitly or implicitly, the economics of manorial housekeeping, since in both cases what is needed is unstintingly provided.

The estate poets find it convenient to "age" their subjects as much as possible; thus Penshurst is "an ancient pile." Not all the manors were so old, nor did those holding tenure at the time of the poem necessarily have such an ancient claim. Penshurst Place, Kent, dates from 1347, but it passed into the Sidney family in 1552; it still survives, much as it was in Jonson's time.[2] Rushden,

---

1 "A Panegerick to Sir Lewis Pemberton," *The Complete Poetry of Robert Herrick,* ed. J. Max Patrick (New York, 1968), p. 199. All citations from Herrick's works from this edition.

2 Penshurst, the seat of Lord De Lisle, was built in 1341–49 by a wealthy former lord mayor of London, Sir John Poulteney. He obtained leave to crenellate the building, but there was never a moat, nor in all likelihood was Penshurst defensible. The great hall dates

the Northamptonshire manor of Sir Lewis Pemberton, which also survives, is a newer place, probably of the sixteenth century, but with a Jacobean or early Caroline façade that may be Sir Lewis' doing.[3] Neither Sir Robert Wroth's house nor the two memorialized by Carew have left a trace. Durrants, in Middlesex, was in the possession

---

from the close of the fourteenth century. Sir John died without male heirs, and the estate passed to Sir John Devereux, constable of Dover and lord warden of the Cinque Ports, who before 1400 added a wing adjacent to the solar. After changing hands several times, Penshurst reverted to the crown during the reign of Henry VIII on the attainder of the Duke of Buckingham, into whose family the house had passed. Edward VI bestowed the estate upon his chamberlain and tutor Sir William Sidney in reward for services done in his father's lifetime. The wing of the 1390s was remodelled under Elizabeth into the present suite of apartments. At the time of Jonson's poem, Penshurst was held by Robert Sidney (brother of Sir Philip), who was made Baron Sidney of Penshurst in 1603, Viscount Lisle in 1605, and Earl of Leicester in 1618; he died in 1626. Lady Sidney, nee Barbara Gamage, is described as "an heiress with extravagant ideas about her household retinue." See Lady de l'Isle and Dudley's notes on Penshurst in *Famous Homes of Great Britain and Their Stories,* ed. A. H. Malan (New York, 1900); L. C. John, "Ben Jonson's 'To Sir William Sidney on His Birthday'," *Modern Language Review,* LII (1957), 168–76; "Penshurst Place, Kent, a Seat of Lord De Lisle and Dudley," *Country Life,* XXX (2 December 1911), 844–54; (9 December 1911), 894–902; and Marcus Binney, "Penshurst Place, Kent," *Country Life,* CLI (9 March 1972), 554–58; (16 March 1972), 618–21; (27 April 1972), 994–98; (4 May 1972), 1090–93.

3 Nikolaus Pevsner, in *The Buildings of England: Northamptonshire* (London, 1961), p. 395, writes of Rushden: "Inside, the arches from the screens passage into the original office quarters survive . . . The centre is a semicircular, two-storeyed embattled bay. The wings have identical bays attached. Doorway to the r. of the middle bay, with a four-centred head. The wings have shaped gables, their tops openwork semicircles." The gables appear to be additions of the 1620s; the rest of the house remains old-fashioned. The irregular position of the doorway is characteristic of early sixteenth-century houses. Sir Lewis, knighted in 1617, became Sheriff of Northamptonshire in 1621; he died in 1640.

of the Wroth family from the late fourteenth century, and the manor itself dates from that period, though it is likely that additions would have been made by Jonson's time.[4]

4 The Wroths, originally from Wrotham (Kent), acquired Durrants, in Enfield parish, in the late fourteenth century. Sir Thomas Wroth, a protege of Warwick, became important at Court under Edward VI. Jonson dedicated *The Alchemist* to Lady Wroth but apparently had a lesser opinion of Sir Robert than his poem suggests (H&S, I, 55). Lady Wroth was Sir Robert (and Sir Philip) Sidney's niece. Sir Robert succeeded to the estate of Durrants in 1606 and died in 1614. See *The Victoria History of the County of Middlesex* (London, 1911), II, 4, 30, 41; and Michael Robbins, *Middlesex* (London, 1953), p. 98.

31. Rushden, the Northamptonshire home of Sir Lewis
Pemberton.

The manor of Little Saxham, near Bury St. Edmunds
(Suffolk), was built in the early sixteenth century and
passed to the Crofts family—the ones Carew knew—in
1531.[5] Apparently even in Carew's day it remained a

5 Sir Thomas Lucas, solicitor general to Henry VII, built the manor
of Saxham at a cost of slightly above £700. On his death in 1531, the
manor passed to the Crofts family, who held it for over two centuries.
Thomas Carew's host was Sir John Crofts (1563–1628), who was
knighted in Ireland in 1599 and had been master at Saxham since
1612. His son, the intended speaker of the poem "To the King at his
entrance into Saxham," traveled with Carew and Lord Herbert of
Cherbury to France in 1619; he was created Lord Crofts in 1658, but

LITTLE SAXHAM IN 1638.

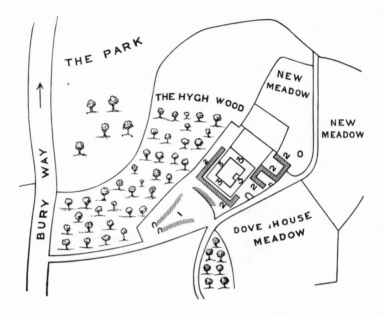

32. Sketch after a 1638 estate map of Little Saxham Manor.
Little Saxham Parish Registers.

quaint structure of the Henry VII period, moated on
three sides and enclosing a courtyard. A 1638 estate map

---

the title died with him in 1677. Carew's editor records an 1844 account
of the hall (pulled down in 1771): "The Hall was one of those
picturesque, brick embattled, manor houses, with towers, irregular
gables, finials, and clusters of ornamental chimneys . . ." (*The Poems
of Thomas Carew,* ed. Rhodes Dunlap [Oxford, 1949] p. 225). A new
suite of apartments had been added under the Restoration for the
reception of Charles II. See also *Little Saxham Parish Registers,
1559–1850,* ed. "S.H.A.H.," Suffolk Green Books, V (Woodbridge,
Eng., 1901); and John Nichols, *The Progresses, Processions, and Magnificent Festivities of King James the First* (London, 1828), III, 587, n.

survives, although the house was pulled down in 1771. The magnificent house of Wrest that is to be seen in Bedfordshire today stands adjacent to the site of the older manor that so delighted Carew. The domain had been in the possession of the de Greys, later earls of Kent, since the late thirteenth century, and the manor in question was built by the first earl before 1490. It was extensively improved in the late sixteenth century.[6]

If these houses do not uniformly boast credentials of great feudal antiquity, they nevertheless date from a period that to Jacobean or Caroline eyes was extremely remote. Despite additions at Rushden, Wrest, and Penshurst (which acquired a splendid Elizabethan wing), the houses fall well within the older traditions of English architecture. All had grown slowly, if at all, and even so large a house as the Sidneys' can be said to have seemed uninsistent and accommodating. Yet they were not merely old houses. All were within easy reach of London, and most played host to King James at least once. Jonson makes an important event of James's visit in "To Penshurst," although the date is not known, and refers obliquely to a similar hunting foray at Durrants ("To Sir Robert Wroth," lines 21–24). I know nothing of a visit to Rushden, but the King was acquainted with Pemberton's

6 Pevsner, in *The Buildings of England: Bedfordshire, Huntingdon, and Peterborough* (London, 1968), p. 172, speaks of an Elizabethan or Jacobean house which stood just to the south of the present structure. But Joyce Godber, in the *History of Bedfordshire, 1066–1888* (Bedford, Eng., 1969), p. 228, believes that Carew is speaking of a fifteenth-century house. Because it is generally agreed that there have been three structures, the second can be no earlier than 1702, and there was a building on the site as early as the 1490s, I think it likely that Pevsner is speaking of a fifteenth-century manor with sixteenth-century additions and perhaps a new façade. See also "Wrest Park, Bedfordshire, the Seat of Earl Cowper," *Country Life,* XVI (1904), 54–65, 90–98.

father. James stopped at Wrest in progress on July 21, 1612, and visited Saxham during the winter of 1619–20, and again in 1621–22. Carew's poem "To the King at his entrance into Saxham" is a speech of fealty to James from the house and its tenants. An interesting aspect of the poem is its insistence that this is a simple country place, able to provide no rare dainties, but only what the season can afford. At the same time, the rites of Old Testament sacrifice are expressed in terms of the offering of food and drink. Carew's poem serves as a nice pendant to "To Saxham," suggesting the degree to which the virtues of simplicity and old manors were given at least lip service.

Our interest in the architectural history of these old estates lies in the comparisons with their spectacular rivals. The gauntlet is flung down by Jonson:

> Thou art not, Penshurst, built to envious show,
>   Of touch, or marble; nor canst boast a row
> Of polish'd pillars, or a roofe of gold:
>   Thou hast no lantherne, whereof tales are told;
> Or stayre, or courts; but stand'st an ancient pile,
>   And these grudg'd at, art reverenc'd the while.
>
> (lines 1–6)

The lantern may be the notorious top story of Wollaton Hall (Nottinghamshire), and in several other points the rival establishment suggests the Temple of Solomon,[7] but otherwise no actual house fits the description. In "Wroth" no other country house is mentioned, but the "proud porches, or their guilded roofes" (line 15) of Vergil and Horace are given as symbols of city life. Herrick's

---

7 See Gayle E. Wilson, "Jonson's Use of the Bible and the Great Chain of Being in 'To Penshurst'," *Studies in English Literature*, VIII (1968), 77–89.

architectural dichotomy is rudimentary; Pemberton's house is easily recognized as old, because of its traditional English plan including "worn Threshold, Porch, Hall, Parlour, Kitchin" (line 5), but its contrary is merely suggested by "Pillars of lasting Jet" and by such subsidiary luxuries as a fretted ceiling or "A Sweating-Closset, to annoint the silke- / soft-skin" (lines 124, 121–22).

Carew does not praise Saxham by contrast with another structure, but he compares Wrest favorably with other houses and fixes the relationship of architecture to domestic virtue:

> Such pure and uncompounded beauties, blesse
> This Mansion with an usefull comelinesse,
> Devoide of Art, for here the Architect
> Did not with curious skill a Pile erect
> Of carved Marble, Touch, or Porpherie,
> But built a house for hospitalitie.[8]

Carew speaks for the genre in insisting on the absence of art, or the incompatibility of artistry and virtue—virtue lying in what is *useful.* Like Jonson, Carew sees in the grander mansions of the day something like Spenser's House of Pride, since it is difficult to believe that he speaks of contemporary building materials with any precision. The rivals of Penshurst Place, like Carew's and Herrick's contrary structures, are moralized buildings, burdened with pride and ambition. Carew's architectural descriptions become somewhat more detailed as he makes the distinction between *being* and *seeming:*

8 "To my friend G. N. from Wrest," in *The Poems of Thomas Carew, with His Masque Coelum Britannicum,* ed. Rhodes Dunlap (Oxford, 1949), p. 87. Subsequent citations from Carew's poetry from the Dunlap edition.

No sumptuous Chimney-peece of shining stone
Invites the strangers eye to gaze upon,
And coldly entertaines his sight, but cleare
And cheerefull flames, cherish and warme him
here:
No Dorique, nor Corinthian Pillars grace
With Imagery this structures naked face . . .

("Wrest," lines 25–30)

The antithesis of the eye to the sense of feeling is that of
being to seeming, life to sterility, substance to image, and
utility to ornament, as well as a "home" to "architecture." The principle of utility is stated explicitly, and in
architectural terms:

Nor thinke, because our Piramids, and high
Exalted Turrets threaten not the skie,
That therefore Wrest of narrownesse complaines
Or Streightned Walls, for she more numerous
traines
Of Noble guests daily receives, and those
Can with farre more conveniencie dispose
Than prouder Piles, where the vaine builder
spent
More cost in outward gay Embellishment
Then reall use: which was the sole designe
Of our contriver, who made things not fine,
But fit for service.

("Wrest," lines 47–57)

Only the existence of a genre of poems of this kind can
explain, I think, such curious praise, and one wonders if
Lady Kent appreciated "things not fine." In any case the
judgment of Pride and Vanity upon the modern mansion

is extended by Carew into a statement on the irrecon-cilability of utility, or excellence, with architecture in a formal sense. Martial hinted at an architectural extrava-gance that merely represented the inner failings of the house of Bassus: Jonson's house of Pride, and Carew's, though of a strongly emblematic nature, are to some degree *designed* to frustrate the ends of an honest house. Presumably the same pride that suggested the "Pillars of jet" and so on is at the bottom of the denial of hospitality, but Carew's "Chimney-peece of shining stone" itself precludes, however irrationally, the warmth of a fire.

Although Martial complained of Bassus' garden, *otiosis ordinata myrtetis,* the English do not follow him in such distinctions. Carew speaks of the "gardens, orchards, walks" of Saxham, and Jonson describes the somewhat old-fashioned gardens of Penshurst, with the Mount, and walks "for health, as well as sport." Beyond these approv-ing glances, however, Jonson and Carew (for Herrick is silent on the subject of the grounds at Rushden) show an admiration for the demesnes around them that in the latter case engenders metaphysics. Penshurst, though not built of precious materials, takes pleasure "in better marks, of soyle, of ayre, / Of wood, of water" (lines 7–8). Carew, somewhat similarly though conceitedly, says of Saxham, "Water, Earth, Ayre, did all conspire, / To pay their tributes to thy fire" (lines 29–30). With obvious pleasure, Jonson dwells upon the landscape at Penshurst, taking us through groves of woods, past the low fields next to the Medway, and back up the hills again; we visit first the fish ponds and then the orchards.

In "To Sir Robert Wroth," Jonson follows his de-scription of the sophisticated pleasures of the hunt with a survey of Wroth's properties.

The whil'st, the severall seasons thou hast seene
    Of flowrie fields, of cop'ces greene,
The mowed meddowes, with the fleeced sheepe,
    And feasts, that either shearers keepe;
The ripened eares, yet humble in their height,
    And furrowes laden with their weight;
The apple-harvest, that doth longer last;
    The hogs return'd home fat from mast;
The trees cut out in log; and those boughes made
    A fire now, that lent a shade!

                        (lines 37–46)

With this nearly pastoral picture Jonson manages to itemize a great deal of the agricultural and livestock resources of Durrants while leading us neatly back to the Hall, for which the cut trees provide fireplace fuel. The passages immediately following are about the feast in the great hall, which is, here as in the other poems of the genre, the terminus both of the poet's survey and of the products of the estate.

    The mutual dependence of master and tenant, and of both upon the land, is the concluding sentiment of Herrick's poem "The Hock-Cart, or Harvest Home." He admonishes the farm-hands:

And, you must know, your Lords word's true,
Feed him ye must, whose food fils you.
And that this pleasure is like raine,
Not sent ye for to drowne your paine,
But for to make it spring againe.

                        (lines 51–55)

Herrick, a gentleman and the friend of Pemberton and of Lord Westmorland (to whom "The Hock-Cart" is addressed), is naturally above the condition of the laboring "sons of summer." But while romanticizing their harvest toil, he still pictures the activities of an English estate and suggests the intimate, though urbane, understanding of the importance of farming that lies at the basis of an appreciation of country-house life. Jonson's discreet pastoralizing of the properties at Durrants and Penshurst reveals like sympathy for the labor done in the fields.

The English estate poets credit agricultural properties and formal gardens with similar virtues, not distinguishing between "real" fields and "artificial" beds of flowers. Carew begins his salute to Wrest with praise of what could be either meadow or garden:

> Here steep'd in balmie dew, the pregnant Earth
> Sends from her teeming wombe a flowrie birth,
> And cherisht with the warme Suns quickning heate,
> Her porous bosome doth rich odours sweate;
> Whose perfumes through the Ambient ayre diffuse
> Such native Aromatiques, as we use
> No forraigne Gums, nor essence fetcht from farre,
> No Volatile spirits, nor compounds that are
> Adulterate, but at Natures cheape expence
> With farre more genuine sweetes refresh the sense.
> (lines 9–18)

These lines introduce us to the architectural passages and foreshadow their praise of "natural" English materials. The rich, productive land is kept in the forefront of the description of the estate; it is the source of the food that figures of necessity in the scenes of communal dining, and the occasion of greatest delight for Carew, who contrasts the warm sun and flowers of Wrest with the brutal climate of the Tweed. It is in the gardens of these houses, and not in their walls, that the Englishman indulges in such luxuries as color and aroma.

The sponte sua Theme

At the basis of the moral and financial economy of the villa of Faustinus one finds the Golden Age principle of spontaneously useful behavior: from vegetable to over-lord, each component of the estate willingly does that which must be done, finding, indeed, fulfillment of identity in performing the act.

Such are the creatures of Penshurst Place, whose voluntary contributions to the general welfare are suggested by passages in Martial (X, 30) and Juvenal (Satire IV: the turbot of Domitian). The fruits of the orchard merely live up to their nature, coming each one in its season (lines 41–42); though they also "hang on thy walls, that every child may reach" (44). Somewhat more enthusiastically, the woods "never fail" to provide deer (20–21), and with a series of active verbs Jonson goes on to praise the land near the river for feeding the animals, the higher ground for breeding horses, the banks for yielding conies, and the woods for providing "the purple pheasant, with the speckled side" (28).

The game and fish, taken more directly from Martial,[9] present themselves with increasing gusto:

> The painted partrich lyes in every field,
> And, for thy messe, is willing to be kill'd.
> And if the high-swolne *Medway* faile thy dish,
> Thou hast thy ponds, that pay thee tribute fish,

9 The painted partridge is the *picta perdrix* of Epigram III, 58, and the self-sacrificing fish are from X, 30.

Fat, aged carps, that runne into thy net.
And pikes, now weary their owne kinde to eat,
As loth, the second draught, or cast to stay,
Officiously, at first, themselves betray.
Bright eeles, that emulate them, and leape on
land,
Before the fisher, or into his hand.
(lines 29–38)

The terminus of this important migration is the table, where one may also find the fruits of the tenants' good will:

But all come in, the farmer, and the clowne:
And no one empty-handed, to salute
Thy lord, and lady, though they have no sute.
Some bring a capon, some a rurall cake,
Some nuts, some apples; some that thinke they
make
The better cheeses, bring 'hem; or else send
By their ripe daughters, whom they would
commend
This way to husbands; and whose baskets beare
An embleme of themselves, in plum, or peare.
(lines 48–56)

The tenants bearing gifts originate in Martial (Epigram III, 58), but Jonson, possibly amused by the mention of the ruddy health of farmers' daughters ("grandes proborum virgines colonorum"), has taken the opportunity to sketch in a picture of plebeian courtship, suggesting also that both the young girls and the provisions are fruits of the estate. Like the vines, woods, fish, and animals, the tenants are drawn to the house to give what is necessary and to take their reward at the "liberall boord"—or

119

presumably so, since Jonson's picture of the hospitality at Penshurst is expressed rather in terms of his own reception than by a picture of the general gathering.

Carew imitates the Jonsonian cycle in "To Saxham," where the season is winter and the tenants' need for relief is more pressing:

> The cold and frozen ayre had sterv'd
> Much poore, if not by thee preserv'd,
> Whose prayers have made thy Table blest
> With plenty, far above the rest.
> (lines 11–14)

The tenants' good will, expressed in their prayers, has caused God to furnish Saxham with the full table that relieves the supplicants; the circle of good deeds makes up a moral economy bounded by the demesne of Saxham. The food required for this system of charity also reflects the general religious imagery of the poem:

> The Pheasant, Partiridge, and the Larke,
> Flew to thy house, as to the Arke.
> The willing Oxe, of himselfe came
> Home to the slaughter, with the Lambe,
> And every beast did thither bring
> Himselfe, to be an offering.
> The scalie herd, more pleasure tooke,
> Bath'd in thy dish, then in the brooke.
> (lines 21–28)

Like Penshurst, Saxham Hall itself is the creature addressed by the poem and is itself the active agent of virtue; preserving the poor, it also attracts the beasts of the estate, as though to bring them to their fulfillment. Saxham is apparently unique in its magnetism; we are told that the neighbors suffer from lack of food, "Yet thou hadst dainties, as the skie / Had only been thy Volarie" (lines 17–18), and the birds are said to seek refuge at Saxham against a new Deluge. The voluntary sacrifice of the animals comes from Martial and Jonson, but the religious details of ark and sacrifice are Carew's own, and they point up his efforts (somewhat strained, perhaps) to etherealize this old manor. In a bit of "metaphysical" verse he sums up the influence of Saxham on Nature:

> Water, Earth, Ayre, did all conspire,
> To pay their tributes to thy fire,
> Whose cherishing flames themselves divide
> Through every roome, where they deride
> The night, and cold abroad.
> (lines 29–33)

In the case of both Penshurst and Saxham, it is stated that the resources are inexhaustible; Wrest, too, has a "free, and unexhausted store" (line 60). Jonson dismisses the tenants' little gifts as an act of love, welcome but not necessary to a house so abundantly supplied, and Carew speaks of Saxham as

> So full of native sweets, that blesse
> Thy roofe with inward happinesse;
> As neither from, nor to thy store
> Winter takes ought, or Spring addes more.
> (lines 7–10)

Saxham transcends the necessities of the seasons and subordinates the rhythms of nature to its own economies. It is only by accepting the system of the manor as a kind of perfection that we can reconcile Saxham as an ark for animals in the storm with Saxham as a groaning board.

Nature is assimilated to the useful arts of "fire" and "dish," and in the same sense the animals are "rescued" from a meaningless death in the snow in order to provide for the estate.

The villa of Bassus had many faults, but the worst was its lack of productivity. Bassus had to send to town for even the simplest fare. "How blest are thou," says Jonson to Sir Robert Wroth, who "canst, at home, in thy securer rest, / Live, with un-bought provision blest" (lines 13–14). The Vergilian motif of *dapes inemptae* has a special importance for Jonson, who in the same poem speaks of "the iewells, stuffes . . . not paid for yet!" (lines 11–12). Living off the products of one's own estate is as important at Durrants, Penshurst, or the other English country houses as it was on the farms of Horace, Juvenal, and Martial; and implicit in the Golden-Age economics of a Saxham or Penshurst is the self-sufficiency of this little world. In several of the English poems, the house is praised because "no Stud, no Stone, no Piece, / Was rear'd up by the Poore-mans fleece" ("Pemberton," lines 117–18), and "there's none, that dwell about them, wish them down" ("Penshurst," line 47). These houses utilize the labor of their tenants and the yield of their fields and woods to right purposes, without imposing upon others' rights or victimizing dependents. Herrick and Jonson associate such manorial benevolence with unostentatious architecture, and Jonson speaks in "To Sir Robert Wroth" of the disinheriting and despoiling of widows and orphans as characteristically modern activities. But the manorial system of production, distribution, and consumption achieves the opposite results, and the agricultural economy of the estate serves as a basis for a system, or economy, of relationship between them.

Good Housekeeping

Hospitality, in the form of food and drink, is the natural expression of the good will made possible by abundance, which is itself the reward of virtuous conduct and good estate management. The poems stress the importance of both beasts and fruits of the field, and their use as food for guests; thus the guests are drawn into the cycle of the estate, and the highest value is set upon entertaining them. "Guests," however, are of several kinds. The most obvious are the tenants, whose presence at mealtime in the great hall makes visible the bonds between the offices and classes of the estate. Jonson, in "To Sir Robert Wroth," colors this reunion with golden hues, "As if in Saturnes raigne it were . . . The route of rurall folke come thronging inne, / (Their rudenesse then is thought no sinne)" (lines 53–54). And "Freedome doth with degree dispense," Jonson says, recalling the Arcadian communism mentioned in Athenaeus and Statius.[10]

Carew's picture of dinner at Wrest is somewhat more like Archbishop Parker's banquet, and more fully "medieval" to a romantic eye:

> They throng with living men, their merry Hall,
> Where at large Tables fill'd with wholsome meates
> The servant, Tennant, and kind neighbour eates.
> Some of that ranke, spun of a finer thred
> Are with the Women, Steward, and Chaplaine fed

10 See also Statius, *Silvae* I, 6, 43–56: una vescitur omnis ordo mensa, / parvi, femina, plebs, eques, senatus: / libertas reverentiam remisit.

With daintier cates; Others of better note
Whom wealth, parts, office, or the Heralds coate
Have sever'd from the common, freely sit
At the Lords Table, whose spread sides admit
A large accesse of friends to fill those seates
Of his capacious circle, fill'd with meates
Of choycest rellish, till his Oaken back
Under the load of pil'd-up dishes crack.

(lines 34–46)

Freedom doth not with degree dispense here, but one would have little cause to complain, in view of the spectacular overflow of abundance. Abundance, indeed, is important to Carew, because it is the "being" that he opposes throughout the poem to the "seeming" of fine architecture. Statuary is another craft that comes under attack; the Lord and Lady, who "delight / Rather to be in act, then seeme in sight" (lines 31–32), adorn their hall with guests rather than with statues. The same is true of the provisions:

Nor, croun'd with wheaten wreathes, doth *Ceres* stand
In stone, with a crook'd sickle in her hand:
Nor on a Marble Tunne, his face besmear'd
With grapes, is curl'd uncizard *Bacchus* rear'd.
We offer not in Emblemes to the eyes,
But to the taste those usefull Deities.
Wee presse the juycie God, and quaffe his blood,
And grinde the Yeallow Goddesse into food.

("Wrest," lines 61–68)

Though he inveighs against emblems, Carew represents hospitality emblematically. His picture is ideal and general, even romantic; and such a meal ritually renews kinship among the members of a household through the ceremonious breaking of bread. A similar situation is implied in the graver poem "To Saxham," where the hall is a refuge, an ark, against a winter that resembles the Deluge.

Besides the tenants, strangers must be entertained. Hall complained (Satire V, 2) of gates closed against strangers. But Carew speaks of the "weary Pilgrim" finding refreshment at Saxham and of a household eager to keep him as a guest. The house itself is again credited with active virtues: "thy gates have bin / Made onely to let strangers in" (lines 51–52), and Herrick, like Carew, speaks of the tangible virtues of a house

> Where laden spits, warp't with large Ribbs of Beefe,
>   Not represent, but give reliefe
> To the lanke-Stranger, and the sowre Swain;
>   (lines 9–11)

The generosity of these houses is apparent in their ease of access. Carew speaks of the gates of Saxham as "untaught to shut," and Herrick says much the same about Rushden. At Saxham, the arrival of even the least desirable sort of guest serves to reaffirm abundance:

> And as for theeves, thy bountie's such,
> They cannot steale, thou giv'st so much.
>   (lines 57–58)

A more important sort of guest, however, is one of that "large accesse of friends" of gentle birth, particularly the poet himself. It is his voice we hear. The Roman poets wrote of inequities and rude treatment at the tables of the rich, but the English poets praise the equity and courtesy of their hosts. Jonson praises Penshurst,[11]

> Where comes no guest, but is allow'd to eate,
>> Without his fear, and of thy lords owne meate:
> Where the same beere, and bread, and selfe-same wine,
>> That is his Lordships, shall be also mine.
> And I not faine to sit (as some, this day,
>> At great mens tables) and yet dine away.
>
> (lines 61–66)

The introduction of this theme of equality or inequality between host and guest is important. It serves to extend the dichotomy between the two sorts of houses from analyses of productivity (or utility) and architectural styles into the area of hospitality, even to the details of the table. Martial praised Faustinus' hospitality but did not dwell on it, and the classical genre of estate poems has little to say about comparative meals. But hospitality is the key quality of the "good" English country house; it is the expression and utilization of the estate's resources, and it is the capital laid out to ensure a return of good will. Jonson turned to other Latin poems, Juvenal's Fifth Satire and several epigrams of Martial, for the twin themes of unequal fare and rude service, and he incor-

---

11 Here Drummond's record of Jonson's words is helpful: "being at ye end of my Lord Salisburie's table with Inigo Jones & demanded by my Lord, why he was not glad My Lord said he yow promised I should dine with yow, bot I doe not, for he had none of his meate, he esteamed only yt his meate which was of his owne dish." The dinner incident probably occurred at Theobalds, according to Jonson's editors, either on 24 July 1606 or on 22 May 1607 (H&S, I, 57, n.). Jonson also told Drummond that "Salisbury never cared for any man longer nor he could make use of him" (H&S, I, 142).

porated them into the estate genre as a basis for distinguishing between good and bad country homes.

The motif of the ungenerous servant runs throughout the English estate poems. Juvenal (Satire V) and Martial (Epigram III, 60; "In Varum") complain of waiters who minister to the host's needs while ignoring or even berating the guests. But Martial's poem to Bassus is the model for Jonson's remark that at the Sidneys' table

>   . . . no man tells my cups; nor standing by,
>   A waiter, doth my gluttony envy:
>   But gives me what I call, and lets me eate,
>   He knowes, below, he shall finde plentie of
>   meate,
>   Thy tables hoord not up for the next day.
>   (lines 67–71)[12]

A stranger at Saxham finds that his welcome increases with his stay, and that "There's none observes (much lesse repines) / How often this man supps or dines" (lines 47–48). Carew associates a porter at the door with the wrong sort of country house, while saying of Saxham, "Thou hast no Porter at the doore / T'examine, or keep back the poor" (49–50). Herrick is pleased that Rushden has no "black-bearded Vigil" who "beats with a button'd-staffe the poor" ("Pemberton," 13–14). He expands the motif of the surly waiter into two long passages on bad table manners, one of which introduces the "rough Groom" who says to the stranger,

>   . . . Sir
>   Y'ave dipt too long i'th Vinegar;

12 Thus Martial: nec avara servat crastinas dapes mensa, / vescuntur omnes ebrioque non novit / satur minister invidere conviviae (Epigram III, 58, 42–44).

And with our Broth and bread, and bits; Sir,
friend,
Y'ave farced well, pray make an end;
Two dayes y'ave larded here; a third, yee know,
Makes guests and fish smell strong; pray go
You to some other chimney . . .

(lines 21–27)

The rude servant in Juvenal and Martial is linked to the vicious custom of serving unequal fare, and it is no doubt an indication of the importance of food and the hospitality of the hall to the English estate poets that rude servants and unequal fare are stressed. At Rushden all "find equall freedome, equall fare" (line 60) and, as at Saxham, guests are encouraged to eat ("Pemberton," lines 61–64). Nothing was said in Martial's estate poem about equality or inequality of food, nor much about the staff's attitude toward guests, but the English poets, principally relying on Juvenal, introduce the twin motifs to flesh out the theme of hospitality. The contrast between well-run and badly-run tables of English country houses follows the pattern of the architectural dichotomy and has the effect of ennobling respectable landlords like Pemberton, whose

. . . choicest viands do extend
Their taste unto the lower end
Of thy glad table; not a dish more known
To thee, then unto any one.

(lines 67–70)

Hospitality being the natural function of a country house, the manner in which food is served becomes of some importance. The community of dishes at Pemberton's table is another reminder of the Golden Age, just as

the technique of praising one thing by dispraising another—in this case, bad servants and bad service—is the
usual approach of poets (like Ovid) describing the Golden
Age. It happens to be Jonson's favorite satirical technique
and perhaps found its way into the estate-poem genre
because he wrote "To Penshurst," especially the passages
on eating, with a satirical emphasis.

Perhaps it was his bad experience at Theobalds that
induced Jonson to associate modern architecture with
bad table manners. His ideal of good manners is the host
who provides "as if thou, then, wert mine, or I raign'd
here," suggesting the absence of *meum* and *tuum*, as in the
first age. Edward Hyde, first earl of Clarendon and one of
Jonson's hosts in later years, wrote of a literary salon that
was perhaps more to Jonson's liking than the "route of
rurall folke": at Lord Falkland's estate of Tew, near
Oxford, dons and Londoners

> all found their lodgings there, as ready as in the
> colleges; nor did the lord of the house know of
> their coming or going, nor who were in his house
> till he cáme to dinner, or supper, where all still
> met; otherwise, there was no troublesome cere-
> mony or constraint, to forbid men to come to the
> house, or to make them weary of staying there, so
> that many came thither to study in a better air,
> finding all the books they could desire in his
> library, and all the persons together, whose com-
> pany they could wish, and not find in any other
> society.[13]

It is of some importance to realize, I think, that
Jonson's execration upon inhospitality is very much a

13 *The Life of Edward, Earl of Clarendon . . . in which is Included A
Continuation of His History of the Grand Rebellion* (Oxford, 1827), I, 48.

denunciation of the bad treatment shown a poet and man of worth like himself, whereas Carew and Herrick are more interested in the large and somewhat archaic canvas of the great hall, with its ranks and classes of diners. An image of meed halls and open central hearths can have meant little to the votary of Horace and Seneca, but the sort of reception he might on his own merits gain at the table of a patron, or in the salon of Lady Bedford at Twickenham, is another thing. Jonson felt that the poet was the counselor of princes, and that probably he had as much to offer the prince's counselor, Sidney, as the nobleman had to give him. In "Penshurst" Jonson asserts his rights within the more archaic framework of manorial hospitality, and justifies a critic's insight that "his poetry, even more than his plays, links seventeenth-century culture and the polite civilization of the Augustans to the better features of the medieval social order and to the half-religious ideal of courtesy."[14]

This personal and rather "modern" touch is absent from the praise of the entertainment at Rushden, Wrest, or Saxham, though something akin to it occurs in the scene of the hunting party at Durrants. This sport, apparently Wroth's principal activity, is done "more for exercise, than fare" ("To Sir Robert Wroth," line 30) and falls rather into the context of upper-class country pleasures than into the workaday business of a manor. Wroth and his "gladder guests" who go "hauking at the river, or the bush, / Or shooting at the greedie thrush" (lines 33–34) enjoy sports foreign to the villa of Faustinus and its descendants and more akin to an aristocratic hunting party today. It is to Jonson's credit that he moves with

14 Geoffrey Walton, *Metaphysical to Augustan: Studies in Tone and Sensibility in the Seventeenth Century* (London, 1955), p. 44.

such ease between the generic conventions and the modern tastes of those whom he addresses. Somewhat in the same manner, he invites friends to dinner in a well-known poem (Epigram CI), at once imitating Horace and Juvenal and insisting upon his own tastes and opinions, likes and dislikes.[15]

Jonson's direct addresses to his subjects, and his satirical and analytical bent, distinguish his two estate poems from those of Carew and Herrick. Jonson goes beyond the demands of the genre to record his feelings about his hosts and about his position as a guest, whereas Herrick is content with effusive praise and Carew remains distant, never identifying the masters of Wrest and Saxham by name or reference (Martial's relationship to Faustinus also is never made explicit). If Herrick and Carew seem to write somewhat from a distance, Jonson, who grumbles, exhorts, and praises with loud damns, seems very much on the spot. He utilizes the conventions to express his praise, but the other poets seem to be bounded by the genre; such an observation is, of course, a commonplace way of defining Jonsonian classicism.

Praise of Patron and Host

A poet is more likely to write in praise of a man than of a building, the prospect of reward being more favorable, and the country-house poets are strongly inclined to put in good words for the masters as well as for the domains. In fact, it is not always of great importance whether the poem be addressed to the house or to the

15 Horace (Satire II, 6) records a meal in the Sabine house, but Juvenal's enjoyment of a similar meal in town (Satire XI) seems approximately parallel to the supper of a confirmed city-dweller.

man. "To Penshurst" and "To Saxham" speak directly to the building, but the former has much to say about the Sidney family; "To Sir Robert Wroth" and "A Panegerick to Sir Lewis Pemberton" are obviously addressed to the man, but both (especially Herrick's poem) are within the genre, work through its conventions, and discuss the life of the manor if not its architecture. "To My Friend G. N. from Wrest" addresses an uninvolved third party but praises Wrest Park itself, while (like "To Saxham") effectively ignoring the hosts. Martial's epigram provided no model, since it was addressed (rather rudely, one feels) to the proprietor of the *rival* establishment, an epistolary device that the English do not employ.

Praise of famous men was a business with Jonson. He exhorts them to noble conduct, or praises them for it, rejoices that they have brought back the Golden Age, compliments them on patronizing poets, laments the decay of the old nobility, and generally places himself in the position of artist and counselor to the realm. He felt that the poet's task was to discover "the exact knowledge of all vertues, and their Contraries; with ability to render the one lov'd, the other hated, by his proper embattaling them" (H & S, VIII, 595). He felt also that the study of poetry was conducive to the daily business of life, "disposing us to all Civill offices of Society." Strongly attached to a few great families, he wrote with an eye to the importance of the person addressed—not particularly for his own profit (although he had no reason to despise advancement), but to fulfill the advisory function of the poet at the level of the high councillors of state. His poems to them suggest several themes that occur in estate poetry. He wrote several commendatory verses to Robert Cecil, whom he did not like but perhaps stood in awe of, and with a better stomach he praised the late William Cecil as a prop of the realm and "the poores full Store-house, and just servants field" (*Underwood*, 30).[16] Lady Wroth is epitomized as a paragon in Epigram CIII, and her cousin Lady Rutland, also nee Sidney, is the virtuous recipient of an epistle in dispraise of modern times (*The Forrest*, XII). It is his constant theme that the present age has decayed from the former and that the crisis is especially severe in high places. Thus these satiric lines, supposedly in the mouth of a scion of a great family:

> Let poore Nobilitie be vertuous: Wee,
> Descended in a rope of Titles, be
> From Guy, or Bevis, Arthur, or from whom
> The Herald will. Our blood is now become
> Past any need of vertue.
> (H & S, VIII, 215).

Believing that the great, established families must continue to be the first servants of the state, Jonson is unhappy to see the bourgeois gaining glory in the wars and calls upon the "Beauchamps, and Nevills, Cliffords, Audleys old" to rouse themselves (H & S, VIII, 214). His two estate poems are to the Sidneys and their connections; they are complemented by several poems to members of the family but especially in praise of Sir Philip.

Jonson's conservative taste in noblemen is connected with his sense of the right use of land. He writes with contempt of women who follow fashion and "Melt downe their husbands land, to poure away / On the close groome, and page, on new-yeeres day" (H & S, VIII, 118). Groyne, who sells his land to buy a whore, is the subject of

16 Cecil's anonymous biographer records in detail the large sums spent for charity and relief of the poor at Theobalds and Burghley; see Francis Peck, *Desiderata Curiosa* (London, 1732–35).

an epigram, and La Foole, in *Epicoene,* may be taken as a type of bad landowner: "I . . . show'd my selfe to my friends, in court, and after went downe to my tenants, in the countrey, and survai'd my lands, let new leases, tooke their money, spent it in the eye o' the land here, upon ladies—and now I can take up at my pleasure" (H & S, V, 176). When Jonson cries out, "What need hath nature of silver dishes?" (H & S, VIII, 606) he reiterates both his contempt for luxurious crafts (like fancy architecture) and his concern over the misuse of wealth. In the case of La Foole, the wealth of an estate serves the ends of vanity, and the great houses of touch and marble mentioned in "To Penshurst" are, by inference (lines 45–47), reared at great cost to the entire community. An estate, to be virtuous, requires a virtuous lord; and virtue can be difficult to maintain if one is, like Wroth, "so neere the citie, and court" ("To Sir Robert Wroth," line 3). The mainstay of an estate is the master's conduct; thus York House is celebrated on Sir Francis Bacon's birthday ("Haile, happie Genius of this antient pile!"), both for its antiquity and for its connection with the honorable services of the Bacon family (H & S, VIII, 225).

It has been maintained that the English estate poets follow a Jonsonian pattern of praising the history of the estate, the ancestors of the master, the lord himself, and the future of the estate as seen in the younger generation of the family.[17] Although the hypothesis is attractive and certainly fits Marvell's "Appleton House," Carew and Herrick have nothing to say about past or future genera-

17 Thus Charles Molesworth defines three topics of the genre: "the founding of the estate, the moral worth of the owner and his social role, the continuance of his estate by the children" ("In More Decent Order Tame: Marvell, History, and the Country-House Poem," diss., State University of New York at Buffalo, 1968, p. 52).

tions; nor does Jonson in "Sir Robert Wroth," while in "Penshurst" he confines his attention to the Sidney family, with no reference to the two-hundred-year history of the estate before it passed to them.[18] One should be wary, then, of attributing too grandiose intentions to these poems. Jonson does construct something like this system; but his praise of past Sidneys does not include the first one of them who held Penshurst, but only (not surprisingly) Sir Philip Sidney, who rarely visited the place. Nevertheless, Jonson celebrates the legend that a nut was planted at the time of Sir Philip's birth and that the resultant tree had much to do with making Penshurst the resort of the Muses and other creatures. It is a handsome compliment that prepares us for another intertwining of park and person in Gamage's copps, named after Lady Sidney, nee Barbara Gamage. We feel, without the point having been pressed, that the Sidneys animate their own landscape, for it is the "copp's . . . nam'd of Gamage . . . / That never failes" to serve "season'd deer" (lines 19–20). This is the last we shall hear of estate history until Marvell.

Although "Penshurst" addresses the house itself in the familiar second person, one easily transfers many of the good qualities of the estate to Lord Sidney himself. The descriptions of hunting, fishing, and grazing, and of the trained fruit trees and orchards, imply constant attention from master and staff; and the table to which all food goes is a social creature. Throughout the poems of the genre, as well as in Martial, praise of such well-ordered estates implies praise of those who hold them. At the same time, there are particular reasons for praising

18 Of the Latin poets, only Apollinaris furnishes a model in "Burgus Pontii Leontii."

the present Sidneys—especially in view of the happy reception of the King and Prince Henry, who stumbled upon the place, it would seem, at the end of a day's hunting. The praise of Lady Sidney's "high huswifery" is of course also praise of Penshurst, but the human element is the deciding factor, for without her diligence Penshurst would have had little to offer. Because of her the house seems to reach out to receive the King and his son:

> . . . they saw thy fires
>   Shine bright on every harth as the desires
> Of thy *Penates* had beene set on flame,
>   To entertayn them;
>
> (lines 77–80)

The royal guests are the last to be cited in the list of those who enjoy Penshurst's bounty, and of course the noblest; the house is measured against that standard of theoretical excellence and found not wanting. Implicit also in the lines "or the countrey came, / With all their zeale, to warme their welcome here" (80–81) is the sentimental picture (although the condition is contrary to fact) of a community together, stretching from king down to country people, gathered around the hearth.

Lady Sidney has other virtues, linked to those of her children. Jonson assigns them in his usual sour way:

> Thy lady's noble, fruitfull, chaste withall.
> His children thy great lord may call his owne:
> A fortune, in this age, but rarely knowne.
>
> (lines 90–93)

But the children are important, because they will replace the parents. Penshurst is the right environment for them, and their education includes prayer with the entire household. It is said that they will continue the traditions of courtliness, martial exploits, and civil accomplishments by imitating their parents; or, as Jonson succinctly puts it, "Reade, in their vertuous parents noble parts, / The mysteries of manners, armes, and arts" (lines 97–98). Jonson's interest in the little Sidneys was genuine enough, though his confidence was misplaced. His rather ambivalent poem of compliment on Sir William's twenty-first birthday in 1611 probably reflects his knowledge of the youth's bad reputation and disgrace at Court.[19] He urges the young man (who died the following year) to maintain the family traditions and live up to their standards. The birthday ode reinforces the passage on the children of Penshurst; in both situations Jonson looks to new generations to merge with the older ones or, in a sense, grow up to be indistinguishable from them in "manners, armes, and arts": a kind of constant "Sidney" is the desideratum. It is questionable to what degree this can be called an historical point of view.[20] Jonson seems rather to want to stabilize the family in one dominant type. Marvell does much the same thing with the Fairfax line.

At Penshurst the threat of a different social order or different way of life remains distant, although one is introduced for purposes of contrast. The Sidneys seem

19 Sir William, born in 1590, stabbed a schoolmaster when he was 15 years old and greatly angered King James. He served in the household of Prince Henry after 1604, preceding him in death by a few weeks. He is buried at Penshurst. See Lisle Cecil John, "Ben Jonson's 'To William Sidney, on His Birthday'," *Modern Language Review*, LII (1957), 168–76.

20 Molesworth says: "The houses are both historical structures and mythical places; historical as records of temporal accomplishment, mythical as preservers of timeless virtues" ("Property and Virtue: The Genre of the Country-House Poem in the Seventeenth Century," *Genre*, I, 2 (April, 1968), p. 152.

secure in their world. "To Sir Robert Wroth," however, is a different sort of poem, hortatory, a bit cautious and doubtful, at times admiring and then upset. It presents the country as an alternative to the city; and were it not specifically about an estate, and did it not work through several of the principle estate-poem generic motifs, "Wroth" would belong more properly to the Horatian or *beatus ille* tradition, which simply offers a rural retreat as an escape from city cares. "Wroth" most closely resembles, in fact, Herrick's "A Country life: To his Brother," which also congratulates someone on his recent rustication. The poem is addressed to Sir Robert rather than to Durrants, but it is the estate that gets the praise, partly for its beauty and productivity (lines 37–46), partly for its maintenance of old English manorial society and its likeness to estates of the Golden Age. Wroth is to be praised only insofar as he bends himself to this rule, to "strive to live long innocent," with the implication that he has had experience of London high life (lines 5–12). The concluding address to Wroth becomes a long tirade on the evils of modern life, war and trade among them, and Jonson continually returns to an imperative mood (with future sense) to urge Wroth to "let others" follow such vain pursuits. Jonson's actual dislike of Wroth may explain the weak figure the man cuts in the poem addressed to him; he has no apparent occupation except hunting, nor any good quality except (and it is somewhat *in potentia*) innocence.[21] But Durrants, which seems to run

---

21 Jonson told Drummond that Lady Wroth was "unworthily married on a Jealous husband" (H&S, I, 142). His relationship with the husband of another patroness, Lady Rutland (nee Sidney) was bad. Jonson, man's man that he is, curiously anticipates the female-dominated society of the seventeenth-century French literary salon.

itself (the scenes in field and hall are presented as fixed tableaux), embodies the virtues that Jonson praises; and he urges Wroth to pursue, not just any sort of country life, but specifically such activities of a country gentleman as the chase.

An estate, then, can be virtuous, excellent, or capable of inducing virtue, independently of its master; indeed, it may be the active agent, and itself serve to improve the master. Jonson attributes such qualities to Durrants by a pastoral treatment of the agricultural and livestock properties of the estate, and by explicitly identifying the communal life of the hall with "Saturnes raigne."

One is frequently struck by Jonson's insistent pessimism. He never tires of accusing his own age of decadence. His "tendency to praise by derision of the opposite"[22] has been well described as having "the force of cynicism beguiled."[23] Lady Sidney's fidelity to her bed, "a fortune, in this age, but rarely knowne," is an example; in a vicious and disordered age (as it seemed to Jonson), a few people of worth must strive to live up to their duties. In his exhortation to Wroth, Jonson names the possible threats to Wroth's innocence and to the sort of life represented by his estate; he speaks of an "ambitious guest / Of Sheriffes dinner, or Maiors feast" (lines 5–6) and denounces the pomp of finery bought on credit (11–12). His dislikes seem to differ little from those of previous centuries; indeed, Marbod wrote of the unpleasantly tumultuous life of twelfth-century Rennes, and both classical literature and several centuries of English dispraise of court life are models for Jonson's poor-

22 Nichols, *The Poetry of Ben Jonson* (London, 1969), p. 123.
23 Rufus A. Blanshard, "Carew and Jonson," *Studies in Philology*, LII (1955), p. 201.

mouthing of London. It should be stressed, I think, how much "Wroth" falls within a convention of dispraise of cities and praise of the retired life, so that the poem will not be read too literally as presenting "threats to the ordered society" in the form of a breakdown of upper-class responsibilities during changing times,[24] or as statement of conservative resistance to new city money and morals. The threats are the old ones—pride, envy, avarice, and anger among them, and ambition in particular.[25]

There is little to say about Carew's or Herrick's praise of host or patron. The Crofts family are not mentioned in "To Saxham," except for the statement to the stranger that he can find a welcome "Both from the Master, and the Hinde." Saxham itself is directly addressed, and its several parts—gates, table, fire—govern active verbs, themselves the agents of virtue. At Wrest, where men rather than statues fill the Hall, we are told that "the Lord and Lady of this place delight / Rather to be in act, then seeme in sight" (lines 31–32), but nothing else is said of them. Carew is more detached from his subject than Jonson; he does not praise his hosts as individuals, nor

24 See Hugh Maclean, "Ben Jonson's Poems: Notes on the Ordered Society," *Essays in English Literature from the Renaissance to the Victorian Age, Presented to A. S. P. Woodhouse,* ed. Millar MacLure and F. W. Watt (Toronto, 1964), p. 45.

25 Besides the opening references to the folly of city life, Jonson attacks the profession of arms (lines 67–72), litigation (73–76), oppression of the weak (77–80), amassing wealth (81–84), and political ambition (85–90). In view of his oft-stated admiration for the martial life (in, e.g., "A Speach According to Horace," "To Sir Henry Cary," "To a Friend, persuading Him to the Warres"), his opposition to it here indicates the extent to which he addresses Wroth in conventional terms; in this case, the conventions are those of the active vs. the retired life, with many qualities of the active life suggesting the *topoi* of the Iron Age.

does he place himself very precisely within the poems. Thus, as one critic has noted, where Jonson says "no waiter doth my gluttony envy," Carew says "There's none observes (much lesse repines) / How often this man sups or dines."[26] His poems are faithful to the conventions of the genre and make no attempt at a Jonsonian immediacy of expression.

Herrick writes directly to Sir Lewis, and has little to say about Rushden except to praise its table; nevertheless, Sir Lewis' golden glow is largely the reflection of his "choicest viands." We know nothing of Sir Lewis' life from the poem; we hear only of his hospitality. Thus, because he sets such a good table, he "[doth] redeeme those times [the Golden Age]," and he is praised for feeding all equally (lines 67–70). Herrick cannot drag himself away from the feast, and he presents Sir Lewis and his wife as models of decorum in their capacity as hosts at dinner (lines 75ff); after the meal they lead a dance, clearly a symbol of the "Ethicks" and "Oeconomicks" of their household. Herrick praises Sir Lewis only in terms of his management of the estate. To the extent that he has built his house rightly ("since no Stud, no Stone, no Piece, / Was rear'd up by the Poore-mans fleece") and has maintained it properly, with lavish and equal hospitality tempered by a just decorum, then to that degree he is "that *Princely Pemberton,* who can / Teach man to keepe a God in man" (lines 133–34). His virtues are functions of the estate and point out the degree to which country-house poetry differs from most panegyrical

26 Blanshard, "Carew and Johnson," p. 201. Blanshard also mentions (p. 203) that the post at Court held by Carew after 1630 might have freed him from the obligations of praising famous men.

verse. The economics of the country house itself furnish the model for good conduct, and the master is subordinated to the larger system of his estate.

The Elevation of the Estate

The imitation of Martial's poem to Bassus marks the transformation of a common sentiment into an ideal. Jonson was not the first Englishman to appreciate the virtues of country-house life. But by placing the country estate within a noble tradition of rural civilization, he established an ideal pattern of country life to which later poets, and their readers, would aspire. The existence of a genre with fixed conventions itself elevates the concept of estate living to a cultural ideal and sets certain values which all estates should take as their goal. By rejecting modern architecture, Jonson identifies the good life on an estate in terms of what is venerably and identifiably English, implying that in homes like Penshurst one finds the flower of English civilization. That his judgments should pursue the question of architecture so intently is not surprising, if hindsight may be used: what Sigfried Giedion calls "the demand for morality in architecture"[27] seems congenial to Anglo-Saxon cultures and has shown itself in such apparently contradictory movements as the Gothic Revival and the Chicago School of the late nineteenth century.

At Penshurst, Durrants, and the other houses, the routine of life is regularly described as an ideal standard; the activities of the estate and the reunions in the hall

27 *Space, Time, and Architecture,* 5th ed. (Cambridge, Mass., 1967), pp. 291ff.

seem divorced from any particular occasion, and are given that timelessness implied by the analogies with the Golden Age. But there are particular ways by which these poets elevate their scene, among them a classicized diction and an array of supernatural creatures. The "Mount" at Penshurst, "to which the *Dryads* doe resort, / Where Pan, and Bacchus their high feasts have made" (lines 10–11),[28] introduces us to the coming feasts in the hall and, with the spirit of Sidney represented by his oak, suggest that the grounds are living, even immortal, and protected by an intelligence; this is more than a garden. At Durrants, the activities of the working part of the estate are slightly pastoralized (lines 37–46), as I have noted, and populated with woodland spirits (47), while the feast in the hall is under the sponsorship of Comus, Apollo, Hermes, Saturn, and the Muses. Pemberton is a Jove in hospitality (61–62) in a house watched over by *genii* and the *lares* (4, 98). At Wrest, the corn and wine are represented to us as the living gods Ceres and Bacchus, and the diners in the hall partake, not of a mere meal, but of the gifts of nature at their fullest. Vertummus and Pomona play in the garden, and the scent of flowers is Flora's answer to the west wind.

The beasts and fishes of the estate were perhaps the most "poetized" elements of Martial's poems on the villa of Faustinus and on the one at Formiae. Jonson adopts the *picta perdrix* as his "painted partrich" and reshapes

28 This passage derives from Martial's Epigram IX, 61, praising a house in Spain or, more specifically, a plane tree in the courtyard called "Caesar's tree": saepe sub hac madidi luserunt arbore Fauni / terruit et tacitam fistula sera domum: / dumque fugit solos nocturnum Pana per agros, / saepe sub hac latuit rustica fronde Dryas. The sense of the poem is that the tree is a guardian spirit of the house because Caesar planted it; Jonson expresses the same idea about the tree planted at Sir Philip Sidney's birth.

Faustinus' barnyard into an extensive property filled with such delights as "the purpled pheasant, with the speckled side" ("Penshurst," line 28); Carew speaks of the "scalie herd" at Saxham (line 27). At Durrants we find "curled woods, and painted meades, / Through which a serpent river leades / To some cool, courteous shade," a picture expanded by Carew to the "spacious channels" that "slowly creepe / In snakie windings" ("Wrest," lines 76–77). Such pastoral language makes something quite noble of ordinary fields and streams.

Jonson and Herrick keep exaggeration within these sober boundaries, but Carew, with his consistently more "metaphysical," conceited, or Donnian turn of phrase, attempts to present the estate as a microcosm of celestial perfection. He hints at such a model in "To Saxham," whose imagery is strongly religious (ark, pilgrim, lambs to the slaughter, the Deluge), and which occupies a unique position of security and detachment, enjoying abundance in the midst of a general famine. Saxham's isolation and self-sufficiency are stressed, and given added force by the confining effects of the snow all around. At Wrest, Carew was apparently struck by the moat surrounding the old house and found in it the occasion to modify his earlier criticisms of the craft represented by statues and architecture:

> Yet we decline not, all the worke of Art,
> But where more bounteous Nature beares a part
> And guides her Hand-maid, if she but dispence
> Fit matter, she with care and diligence
> Employes her skill . . .

Carew distinguishes himself from Jonson and Herrick in considering the proper role of the artisan's craft (rather than dwelling upon its misuse) and is consistent with

them, I think, in permitting a high degree of "art" to the
grounds while denying it to the buildings. He goes on:

> . . . for where the neighbour sourse
> Powers forth her waters she directs their course,
> And entertaines the flowing streames in deepe
> And spacious channells, where they slowly creepe
> In snakie windings, as the shelving ground
> Leades them in circles, till they twice surround
> This Island Mansion . . .

To this point we have a pretty but somewhat pur-
poseless *divertissement* on the subject of the moat—one
which does serve, however, to ennoble the vista of the
estate. Carew then reaches his extravagant climax:

> This Island Mansion, which i' th' center plac'd,
> Is with a double Crystall heaven embrac'd
> In which our watery constellations floate,
> Our Fishes, Swans, our Water-man and Boate,
> Envy'd by those above, which wish to slake
> Their starre-burnt limbes, in our refreshing lake,
> But they stick fast nayl'd to the barren Sphear,
> Whilst our encrease in fertile waters here
> Disport, and wander freely where they please
> Within the circuit of our narrow Seas.
>
> > (Lines 69–88)

One hears of gifts that "it's the thought that counts," and
certainly the idealization of Wrest as the eighth sphere is
an impressive thought, however bizarre. The image seems
gratuitous, with no reference to the values already
praised, nor expressive itself of any precise good quality
that estate might possess. Carew does convey, or makes
clear his intention of conveying, a picture of the estate as a
little cosmos, not dependent upon the outside world and

in fact quite superior to it. The notion (adumbrated in "To Saxham," where, more restrained, it is more successful) is an extension, in the metaphysical mode, of the idealizing tendency implicit in all the poems of the genre. Carew's is certainly the most daring claim made for a country house before Marvell set to the task of memorializing Nunappleton.

5

Marvell and Later Poets

THE CURRENT popularity of "Upon Appleton House," Marvell's long poem on Lord Fairfax' Yorkshire estate, arises not from its celebration of conventional rural excellencies, although that is present, but from its deformation of the language of praise into idiosyncratic meditations on society, nature, and art. The thirty-five stanzas through which we survey the meadows and woods are, like the story of Thwates's close call with the nuns, an extension of generic motifs, but so swollen and elaborated that they take the center of the stage. Ingenious explications of these rich passages, for which "The Garden" and the Mower poems are better analogues than "To Penshurst," obscure our perception of the controlling framework of an estate poem. In dealing both with that framework (itself deformed, though recognizable) and with the idiosyncratic solitariness and obsession with the grounds that distinguish Marvell's speaker from those of other country-house poems, I shall offer no hermetic keys or political allegories, but rather define the generic limits of the estate poem, and suggest in what ways Marvell's peculiar vision of the fruitful manor takes advantage of a cultural and literary enthusiasm for retirement in nature that Jonson would not have encouraged.

Solitude and Gardens

Abraham Cowley is often a convenient index to the intellectual trends of mid-seventeenth century England, perhaps because he states in a general way what other poets, like Marvell, attempt to render more subtly and cryptically. In his poem "Of Solitude," he addresses country houses:

> Hail, the poor Muses' richest manor-seat!
>> Ye country houses and retreat,
>> Which all the happy gods so love,
> That for you oft they quit their bright and great
>> Metropolis above.[1]

Retirement of the Horatian kind, based on a rejection of city life, is Cowley's text; he translates the "Beatus ille" epode and affirms the excellence of simple architecture in a translation of Horace's Epistle I, 10:

> Would I a house for happiness erect,
> Nature alone should be the architect,
> She'd build it more convenient, than great,
> And, doubtless, in the country choose her seat.
> (p. 60)

Elsewhere, Cowley says that country life has ceased to be a condition of necessity because honors and wealth are now gained in the city (p. 39); but he idealizes agriculture as a pursuit and recommends an academy to teach it. The thrust of his remarks is that country life is an ideal occupation for a cultivated man, rather than the elemen-

---

1 *The Essays of Abraham Cowley, with Life,* ed. Dr. Hurd (London, 1868), p. 29. Subsequent references from this edition.

tary condition of most of mankind, and that "necessity," or the gaining of a living, is characteristic of cities. The idea is familiar in Horace, but it had, since Jonson's time, gained a new meaning in Europe.

The development of the theme of solitude in French literature and its transference to England, and especially to Marvell's circle, has been examined in some detail by Bradbrook.[2] Montaigne and Guez de Balzac both recommend retirement as an antidote to ambition, the former noting that "il se faut reserver une arriere boutique toute nostre, toute franche [libre], en laquelle nous establissons nostre vraye liberté et principale retraicte et solitude."[3] Balzac speaks of the retired valley where he lived as "un petit rond tout couronné de montagnes, ou il reste encore quelques grains de cet or dont les premiers siècles ont été faits."[4] It is interesting that Balzac links simple architecture to the retired life in terms like those of the estate poets: "Je ne veux pas vous faire le portrait d'une maison, dont le dessin n'a pas été conduit selon les règles de l'architecture, et la matière n'est pas si précieuse que le marbre et le porphyre" (p. 63).

The idealization of retirement affects both the topography and the metaphysics of estate poetry. Saint Amant, the French *libertin* poet whose "La Solitude" directly influences "Upon Appleton House" (and which was translated by Lord Fairfax, Marvell's employer), treats landscape sympathetically, as an extension of his mood,

---

2 M. C. Bradbrook, "Marvell and the Poetry of Rural Solitude," *Review of English Studies,* XVII (1941), 37–46.

3 "De la Solitude," *Essais,* ed. Maurice Rat (Paris: Garnier, 1962), I, 271.

4 "Lettre a M de la Motte-Aigron" (4 Sept. 1622), in *Seventeenth Century French Prose and Poetry,* ed. Henri Peyre and Elliott M. Grant (Boston, 1937), p. 63.

and as an object of interest because of its purely visual qualities. He provides a model for Marvell's wanderings around the grounds of Appleton and for his extension of the physical features of the estate into metaphysical conceits. Between Saint Amant and Marvell lie the modifying influences of Mildmay Fane, lord Westmorland, and his brother-in-law Fairfax (both of whom translated or imitated Saint Amant), and of Thomas Stanley, another translator of Saint Amant who was connected with the Fairfax family (Bradbrook, p. 38).

Several poems that precede "Upon Appleton House" praise estates for the beauties of their grounds and the contentment afforded by their secluded situation. Don Cameron Allen suggests that the estate poems of Statius and Apollinaris are the models, and that they are therefore the ultimate sources of Marvell's poems.[5] One is a Latin poem by Sarbiewski (1595–1640), translated into English in 1646, about the estate of the Duke of Bracciano. Primarily a topographical description, the ode surveys a vast domain and peoples it with creatures of mythology. Sarbiewski says nothing about the house itself, or the life of the estate, except to mention such pleasures as walking and hunting, which reinforce the poem's emphasis on the estate as a retreat from the court and the city.[6] Georges de Scudéry's "Description de la Belle Maison de Monsieur de Balzac" does not mention the building, but undertakes to praise the solitary sage by subjecting the splendid landscape around him to the influence of Balzac's intelligence. The union of nature

5 *Image and Meaning: Metaphoric Traditions in Renaissance Poetry* (Baltimore, 1960), pp. 122–24.

6 *The Odes of Casimire Translated by G. Hils,* ed. Maren-Sofie Roestvig, Augustan Reprint Society, No. 44 (Los Angeles, 1953), pp. 105–21.

and art found in Balzac's gardens expresses the mind that, "comme un Iardin fertile, / Mesle & confond tousiours le plaisant à l'utile."[7]

Saint Amant's somewhat frivolous poem "Le Palais de la Volupté" is written "sur une maison de plaisance que Monseigneur le Duc de Rets a fait bastir dans la forest de Prinçay" (near Nantes), and possibly provides the source for the work of the "forrain Architect" criticized in "Appleton House" (stanzas i–iv). The Duke's house, or hunting lodge, is quite grand, "et le dessein en chasque part / s'y rapporte aux regles de l'art;" and the poet is enthusiastic about "la salle grande et somptueuse / autant qu'elle est majestueuse."[8] The house is meant for retreat, but of a courtly kind, although "l'estude" is provided for in the library. What may have attracted Marvell's attention (and displeasure), as suggested by the parallel of

> Icy la mesme symmettrie
> A mis toute son industrie
> Pour faire en ce bois escarté
> Le palais de la Volupté
> (Saint Amant, p. 46)

to

> But all things are composed here
> Like Nature, orderly and near,[9]

7 *Poésies Diverses* (Paris, 1649), p. 221.

8 Saint Amant [Marc-Antoine de Gérard], *Oeuvres Poétiques,* ed. Léon Vérane (Paris: Garnier, 1930), p. 46.

9 "Upon Appleton House, to my Lord Fairfax," *The Poems and Letters of Andrew Marvell,* ed. H. M. Margoliouth, 3rd ed., rev. Pierre Legouis and E. E. Duncan-Jones (Oxford, 1971), I, 63. Subsequent citations from Marvell's poems from this edition.

is Saint Amant's contempt for the wild woods ("ces masses enormes / Ou s'entre-confondent les formes, / Ou l'ordre n'est point observé") and his admiration of the "artistic" qualities that isolate the building from the surroundings. A like appreciation of splendid architecture occurs in de Viau's "La Maison de Sylvie," which Marvell probably knew in the greatly abridged 1651 translation by Thomas Stanley entitled "Sylvia's Park." The English title is accurate, because we hear little of the house except a reference to "this proud structures daz'ling Hight,"[10] but much is said about the grounds, which submit to Sylvia's influence and are tamed by her gaze (lines 115–17). J. B. Leishman links "Sylvia's Park" to Waller's "At Penshurst" as examples of the genre of the poem of feminine compliment, and cites them both as the source for the stanzas in praise of Maria in "Appleton House."[11] It is interesting to note that both the de Viau-Stanley work and another poem by Waller contain the classical motif of the self-sacrificing fish.[12]

Mildmay Fane (the patron referred to in Herrick's "Hock-Cart, or Harvest Home") stands closest to Marvell both in many textual parallels and in his manner of surveying an estate. His poem "To Sir John Wentworth, upon his Curiosities and Courteous entertainment at Summerly in Lovingland"[13] has little to say about buildings but much about the park of the estate. There are Jonsonian touches, like the "useful Ash, and sturdy Oak," but the brambles, that "embracing twine int'

10 Thomas Stanley, *The Poems and Translations,* ed. G. M. Crump (Oxford, 1962), p. 157.

11 *The Art of Marvell's Poetry* (London, 1966), pp. 235–37.

12 "There I beheld the Fishes strife, / Which first should sacrifice its life, / To be the Trophey of her Hook" (Stanley, p. 159). See also Waller's "Upon a Lady's Fishing with an Angle."

13 *Otia Sacra, Optima Fides* (London, 1648), p. 153.

Arbours," are closer to the amorous vegetables of Marvell's fantasies. The poem's text is essentially the praise of a gentleman, but much like the poems of the country-house genre (to which it has some claim), it praises the man by praising his surroundings. The deities of pastoral are incorporated into Summerly, and the hospitality of the hall is given a Marvellian importance by association with cosmic order. More detail is lavished upon the gardens. "Earth here's Embroydered into Walks," and a sun dial and wind gauge are seen to harmonize the garden with the elements. Fane ultimately carries us beyond the boundaries of the estate to its larger equivalents in metaphysics: "Now as contracted vertue doth excell / In power and force, This seems a Miracle," he says of the estate, and identifies it as the home of a tenth Muse who could "Court the Soil, with so much Art applide / That all the world seems Barbarous beside." What he has done, as Kitty Scoular notes, is to establish the estate as a microcosm, with all nature's wonders "in Epitome."[14] This inclusion of metaphysical abstraction in the praise of objects provided a model for "Appleton House."

That Fane and Marvell both dwell upon gardens is typical of the age. The earlier poets of the country-house genre never extended their architectural antipathies to the highly stylized gardens of the sixteenth and seventeenth centuries, differing in this from Martial; and in fact the English poets implicitly associate interest in gardens with a correct, or sober, outlook on buildings. Cowley says in the preface to "The Garden" that his wish is to "be master at last of a small house and large garden" (*Essays,* p. 65), probably in imitation of Horace and his

14 *Natural Magic: Studies in the Presentation of Nature in English Poetry from Spenser to Marvell* (Oxford, 1965), p. 163.

Sabine farm. In the poem itself he expresses the commonplace notion that "God the first garden made, and the first city Cain" (p. 69). John Evelyn, to whom Cowley's poem was dedicated, wrote to Sir Thomas Browne that "caves, grotts, mounts, and irregular ornaments of gardens do contribute to contemplative and philosophicall enthusiasme; how *elisium, antrum, nemus, paradysus, hortus, lucus, &c,* signifie all of them *rem sacram et divinam;* for these expedients do influence the soule and spirits of man, and prepare them for converse with good angells; besides which, they contribute to the lesse abstracted pleasures, phylosophy naturall and longevitie . . ."[15] Evelyn also expressed in *Kalendarium Hortense* (1679) the commonplace feeling that gardens were an image of the prelapsarian state.[16] At the time of the Civil Wars, it was equally natural to picture England as the postlapsarian garden—thus Fane's "Anglia Hortus" and "Upon the Times".

"Upon Appleton House" is a product of topographical poetry and the enthusiasm for solitude and gardens as much as it is a continuation of the country-house genre. In the context of Marvell's other poems, "Upon Appleton House" is not extraordinarily complex and idiosyncratic, but within the terms of its genre it is both. The genre asserts itself most fully in this poem as a vehicle for praise of a virtuous person (or persons), rather than as a statement about the social function of country houses.

15 "Letter to Sir Thomas Browne" (28 Jan. 1657 / 58), *Sir William Temple Upon the Garden of Epicurus, with other XVIIth Century Garden Essays,* ed. Albert F. Sieveking (London, 1908), p. 176.

16 See George Williamson, "The Context of Marvell's 'Hortus' and 'Garden'," *Modern Language Notes,* LXXVI (1961), 590–98, and Nicholas A. Salerno, "Andrew Marvell and the *Four Hortensis,*" *SEL,* VIII (1968), 103–20.

Marvell praises one thing by dispraising the opposite, in the traditional manner of estate poems, and outlines his intentions in an earlier and much shorter poem to the master of Nunappleton.

"Upon the Hill and Grove at Bill-borow. To the Lord Fairfax."

With its Latin companion, "Epigramma in Duos montes Amosclivum Et Bilboreum. Farfacio," the English poem on Bilborow equates the physical features of an estate with the moral qualities of its master, Lord Fairfax. Bilborow, a low hill, represents Fairfax's humility (he had retired from Cromwell's service), while Almscliff, a hill of "hook-shoulder'd height" (Marvell, Margoliouth ed., line 11) represents the contrary. The tendency to epitomize, noted in connection with Fane's poem, is an important aspect of "Bill-borow," where the hill "seems as for a Model laid, / And that the World by it was made" (lines 7–8). Its virtues are quietness, courtesy, and accessibility, while the vices of Almscliff are pride, assertiveness, and wrath; so far from epitomizing nature, Almscliff, "For whose excresence ill design'd, / Nature must a new Center find," dislocates the order around it.

The relationship between Fairfax and the hill is more complex than that of analogy. The grove of trees atop Bilborow testifies to Fairfax's presence and influence:

> For something alwaies did appear
> of the *great Masters* terrour there:
> And Men could hear his Armour still
> Ratling through all the Grove and Hill.
> (lines 37–40)

Praise of Fairfax becomes praise of his household, the master and his wife being the guardian spirits of the grove (lines 41–42) where the name "Vera" is cut into the bark. The trees are thus a living memorial of the Fairfax-Vere household and in the rustle of the branches their names are whispered (stanzas vii–viii). The poem returns to the theme of the ambitious and the humble life (stanzas ix–x), identifying the groves of Bilborow as successors to the laurels of war. The grove of trees actually thrives because of Fairfax, or under the influence of "The Genius of the house":

> Hence they successes seem to know,
> And in their *Lord's* advancement grow;
> But in no Memory were seen
> As under this so streight and green.
>
> (lines 53–56)

Marvell has already hinted that the hill, and Fairfax by extension, is no passive exemplum of virtue but active in a mysterious way; it "strives to raise the plain" (line 24). Bilborow prefigures Maria Fairfax.

Like several of the estate poems, "Bill-borow" approaches its human subject by way of topography and surroundings, saying little directly about Fairfax himself. Marvel, differs from Carew, Jonson, or Martial, however, in speaking of a moral virtue (humility) and a state of existence or state of mind (retirement, or withdrawal), rather than of the social virtue of utility (or hospitality). The radical distinction to be made between "Appleton House" and its predecessors lies in its praise of the order of Lord Fairfax's mind and soul, rather than of his customary behavior or the routine of his household.

33. Nunappleton House,
Yorkshire.

"Appleton House:" The Architecture and Gardens

Appleton House (Yorkshire) was begun by Lord
Fairfax's grandfather in 1637 and completed shortly
before the time of Marvell's poem; contrary to the
assumption of many who have written about the verses,
the house was neither modest nor old. Like most Caroline
houses, it attempted little new in design beyond the styles

157

of the 1620s and, according to the woodcut in Clements Markham's *Life of the Great Lord Fairfax,* was a conservatively styled structure with a large central mass and two projecting wings. A porch projects from the middle of the central block, and the wings have square bays on the court. The roof is ornamented with stepped gables, in the Dutch style, and the corners have stone quoins. A cupola surmounts the hall (150 feet long), which was adorned with shields bearing the family arms. "In the other rooms there were chimney pieces of delicate marble of various colours, and many fine portraits on the walls."[17] The central block still stands.

Marvell praises Appleton House in terms that are commonplaces of the genre: the house is "this sober frame." There are several contrary structures. One is the "proud Cawood Castle" of stanza xlvi, an Almscliff to a Bilborovian Appleton and seat of the Archbishop of York. Fairfax's martial flowers, emblems of his humility, seem artillery to demolish "th' Ambition of its Prelate great." Cawood is introduced once as a structure symbolizing the world Fairfax has left, and it is not mentioned again. The old convent of Nunappleton, the ruins of which are on the grounds of the estate, is a more important architectural rival, representing the historical forces that the Fairfaxes have overthrown and replaced with the new house. Its vices are institutional rather than architectural, although "vice infects the very Wall" (line 216). It is an evil house (stanzas xxvii–xxviii), and it vanishes like a wicked fairy's castle (stanza xxxiii) at the Dissolution; its successor, a secular Nunappleton, is the true "religious house" (line 280). A clearer architectural dichotomy, however, is set

17 *A Life of the Great Lord Fairfax* (London, 1870), p. 366.

up within conventional generic terms and pursued through the first ten stanzas.

Several generic motifs are employed to establish the contrast. We are not, "within this sober frame," to expect the work of a foreign architect, by which Marvell may refer to the Flemings Isaac and Salomon de Caux and Balthasar Gerbier (or to Flemish masons who also worked in England). Or, he may mean foreign buildings, like the Escurial of the parallel comparison in Hall's satire, or the "palais de la volupté" praised by Saint Amant. The extravagance of such architecture is described in terms like those of Jonson, Herrick, and Carew—a "hollow Palace" and a "marble crust" are in the vein of "polish'd Pillars"—and just as imprecisely connotative of wicked ostentation. Marvell criticizes the architect (rather than the owner, as Jonson does in "To Penshurst," lines 101–102), shifting emphasis from the vulgar desire to live splendidly to the more philosophic desire to translate extravagant fancy into concrete form. This unnamed house is the work of the architect,

> Who of his great Design in pain
> Did for a Model vault his Brain,
> Whose Columnes should so high be rais'd
> To arch the Brows that on them gaz'd.
> (lines 5–8)

His offenses are several, as, implicitly, are the offenses of the building. One is Pride. Marvell describes a House of Pride, built by one "That thinks by Breadth the World t'unite / Though the first Builders fail'd in Height" (lines 23–24). Besides repeating the error of Babel, the architect "That unto Caves the Quarries drew, / And Forrests did to Pastures hew" (3–4) abuses nature; the theme is

familiar in Marvell.[18] Both sorts of objections imply a
sense of the right relationship between a man and his
environment, specifically his home; and, through the
architectural imagery that equates Fairfax with his house,
Marvell defines his patron's characteristic virtue of humility. Humility expresses itself in just proportions:
"Why should of all things Man unrul'd / Such unpro-
portion'd dwellings build?" (9–10). The animals of stanza
ii exemplify proportion; they are well served by their nests
and shells. The tortoise, whose house is its body, probably
derives (as Kitty Scoular establishes in *Natural Magic*)
from George Wither's fourteenth emblem, showing a
country cottage with a turtle in the foreground.[19] Wither,
like Marvell, favors modest housing and is contemptuous
of one who "in his Hall or Parlour dines, / Which
fret-worke Roofes, or costly Cedar Lines." Fairfax has
understood nature's lesson. He is aware that life is
fleeting, and that he must not show arrogance before the
world or God; his awareness is at least implicit by contrast
in Marvell's rhetorical question, "What need of all this
Marble Crust / T'impark the wanton Mote of Dust?"
(21–22).

In dwelling upon the relationship between man's
physical size and his habitation, and between his ingenu-
ity and a proper sense of his relationships with God and
the natural world, Marvell departs from the societal
assumptions of the country-house genre. Like his predecessors, he defines a virtuous house in terms of its
appropriateness and utility; but the ends to which the
house and its master's life are directed are religious rather

18 Thus in "A Dialogue Between the Soul and Body" Marvell
writes: "So Architects do square and hew, / Green Trees, that in the
Forest grew."

19 Wither, *A Collection of Emblemes* (London, 1635).

than ethical and concern man's spiritual rather than social obligations. Fairfax's retirement expresses his peculiar virtue of humility, and Marvell defines the virtue through its visible equivalent, the house (and estate) that is the place of retirement. This seat, where "all things are composed . . . / Like Nature, orderly and near" (lines 25–26), is not particularly functional, on the model of Penshurst, but is rather an emblem of the right use of materials and of intelligence, like the well-accommodated tortoise. The connection between Fairfax's mind and the style of the building is clear: "Humility alone designs / These short but admirable Lines." What is less clear is the effect of Fairfax's virtue upon the life of the

34. Nunappleton: The south (garden) front.

estate, a matter that is disposed of in stanza ix. The equivalence of the man and the building is the main idea—an equation stressed in the analogy of circle and quadrature (stanza vi) and in the proposition that "holy Mathematicks can / In ev'ry Figure equal Man."

One critic has pointed out that Marvell's extravagant conceits do not accord very well with his arguments in favor of the plain style, at least in architecture.[20] Among these images, that in stanza vii has struck many as particularly odd:

> Yet thus the laden House does sweat,
> And scarce indures the *Master* great:
> But where he comes the swelling Hall
> Stirs, and the *Square* grows *Spherical*;
> More by his *Magnitude* distrest,
> Then he is by its straitness prest:
> And too officiously it slights
> That in it self which him delights.

T. S. Eliot commented that the image, "whatever its intention, is more absurd than it was intended to be";[21] others have understood a reference to the cupola. I agree with Ann Berthoff that the image is purely verbal: "The '*Square* grows *Spherical*' probably derives not from the architectural details of Appleton House but from the

20 According to Robin Grove: "The image of Nunappleton as a 'sober frame' to hold the 'wanton mote of dust,' which the opening stanzas evoke, is curiously irrelevant to what we feel as the life and interest of the poetry; that is, the swiftly changing metaphors and the surprising wit dissolving each conceit into its successor. Verse such as this does not prompt us to an understanding of the various tendencies (humility and naturalness, for instance) that Nunappleton is said to represent" ("Marvell," in *Andrew Marvell: A Critical Anthology*, ed. John Carey [London, 1969], p. 296).

21 *Homage to John Dryden* (n. pub., n.d.), p. 230.

implicit suggestions of the metaphor of the anthropomorphic house, which in turn is based not upon appearance but upon idea."[22]

Stanza vii reveals the strategy of much of the poem. Lord Fairfax's retirement and the humility implied by it give life and meaning to the estate, and determine the qualities for which it shall be praised. Marvell actually exaggerates the simplicity of the manor; the term "sober frame" is more applicable to Fairfax than to Appleton House, and at times the man and the building are described simultaneously.

> So Honour better Lowness bears,
> Then That unwonted Greatness wears.
> Height with a certain Grace does bend,
> But low Things clownishly ascend.
>
> (lines 57–60)

The manor is thus more a state of mind than a household. The simplicities of Penshurst were structural ("thou standst an ancient pile") and socially useful, in that the old hall supported a rural, old-fashioned community. Marvell disposes of these generic motifs of hospitality and patronage in two little emblems in stanza ix. They recall Carew's description of the hall at Wrest, thronged with people rather than statues:

> A Stately *Frontispice of Poor*
> Adorns without the open Door;
> Nor less the Rooms within commends

---

22 Berthoff, *The Resolved Soul: A Study of Marvell's Major Poems* (Princeton, 1970), p. 17. Marvell similarly conflates a man and his habitation in "Flecknoe," lines 83ff: "He drest, and ready to disfurnish now / His Chamber, whose compactness did allow / No empty place for complementing doubt, / But who came last is forc'd first to go out . . . "

Daily new *Furniture of Friends.*
The House was built upon the Place
Only as for *a Mark of Grace*;
And for an *Inn* to entertain
Its *Lord* a while, but not remain.

"Frontispice of Poor" and "Furniture of Friends," besides carrying little weight in a poem whose other images are usually far more striking and complicated, are reductive and pictorial, purposely generalized. They maintain the architectural (or decorative) dichotomy by contrasting a piece of ornamental stonework to a group of dependents, and furniture to human beings. But the gesture is formal, and having fulfilled the generic requirement, Marvell drops the subject.

Marvell is more interested in locating Appleton along the route to heaven. The house, as Fairfax said in similar verses, is a temporary shelter and must give way before the greater house to come. In stanza v, Marvell speaks of Fairfax and his wife as saints, and of Appleton as a future shrine. The masters of the house are clearly headed for a more important domicile; and Appleton itself, unlike previous houses in the genre, is put in its place.

The gardens also express Fairfax's character, and they allegorize his career. Military gardens were a common motif in literature, and Marvell's "*Regiment* . . . of the Tulip Pinke and Rose" (lines 311–12) is not so different from "ces nombreux Escadrons; ces innocens Troupeaux" of flowers that Scudéry describes around Balzac's house. The stanzas about the garden at Appleton (xxxvi–xlvi) praise the retirement of a military man who "did, with his utmost Skill, / *Ambition* weed, but *Conscience* till" (lines 353–54) and invite comparison with the ode on Cromwell, who left off gardening for the wars. In both instances, gardening is an inherently excellent pursuit, a retired equivalent of public virtues, and a type of prelapsarian activity. Thus England, in stanzas xli–xliii, is the "Garden of the world ere while, / Thou *Paradise* of four Seas," although it is now fallen from that state of grace because of war. Marvell digresses somewhat fancifully on the possibility of a nation whose only arms are flowers, but returns eventually to his connected arguments that ambition must be changed for humility and war for gardening. The cultivation of "Conscience" puts Fairfax within, or near, the heavenly garden, and yields the "Flowrs eternal, and divine, / That in the Crowns of Saints do shine" (lines 359–60). These are the military flowers that assault Cawood Castle (stanza xlvi). The wit and serenity associated with the sunlit garden stand in contrast to the sinister designs of the old convent and the nuns; the garden is a stage in the progress from bad house to good house. At the same time, the Paradise of England, whatever its location in history (and too easy an identification with England before 1642 hardly explains the presence of Laud), is associated, if only by juxtaposition in the poem, with the Fairfax-Thwates regime at Appleton.

The Praise of a Patron

Of the several themes of the estate-poem genre, none is more important in "Appleton House" than praise of the lord of the manor. Although the house was a new building, the Fairfaxes had acquired the property at the Dissolution. The story of Thwates and of the sophistries that nearly undid her has been adequately examined in most discussions of this poem; within the terms of the genre, however, the convent episode adds to the praise of the master the dimension of historical and dynastic memorializing. I know of no evidence that Marvell had read Sidonius, although D. C. Allen (*Image and Meaning*) and J. B. Leishman (*The Art of Marvell's Poetry*) suggest that the "Burgus Pontii Leontii" is a model for "Appleton House" because it celebrates the foundation of an estate. The nunnery is the historical antithesis of Appleton House, and its architecture also receives the impression of the character of its inhabitants. An earlier Fairfax, whose good qualities are conflated with those of his descendant, accuses the convent, "vice infects the very Wall" (line 216), and predicts the necessary collapse: "But sure those Buildings last not long, / Founded by Folly, kept by Wrong" (lines 217 / 218). Thwates's suitor, who (somewhat anachronistically) opposes Protestant good sense to Catholic superstition, founds the present house on his marriage and on the stones of the nunnery he acquired afterwards. Both the new Protestant religion and the justice of Fairfax's marriage to Thwates make Nunappleton at last a true "religious house." The distinction between the earlier hero and the later one is blurred, especially when, in the midst of the mock-heroic attack on the convent, Marvell declaims, "Is not this he whose Offspring fierce, / Shall fight through all the *Universe*," and so on (stanza xxxi). Marvell's employer is situated by this device within a tradition of heroic yet pious behavior, and his estate is sanctified (as the nuns' was corrupted) by the quality of his conduct.[23]

23 The history of the convent seems to justify Fairfax's and Marvell's accusations. Founded ca. 1150, the nunnery was subjected to a financial examination after a scandal in 1281. At that time the Archbishop of York ordered that "no one was to be received as nun or sister of the house, or even to live there, without the Archbishop's

Praise of the Fairfaxes is interrupted by the intriguing passage through the meadows and woods, a startling elaboration of the generic survey of the grounds of the estate. Marvell differs most radically from his predecessors in not subordinating the walkabout to the larger theme of estate management. Jonson, in particular, followed his quasi-pastoral descriptions of the grounds and animals with an evaluation of their function, which was to furnish the table and fuel the cycle of hospitality. In outline, Marvell's survey is similar; he leads us from the house through the properties and back to the house ("let's in" are the next-to-concluding words). But we do not really return; there are no scenes of the hall, no entertainment, no talk of food and drink and table manners. The harvest, which is the principal—in fact, the sole—estate activity described is the subject of a complex meditation on the progress of the seasons on cultivated land,[24] well analyzed as a masque by Mrs. Berthoff.[25]

---

special licence, but honest hospitality for a day or night was not meant to be forbidden, so that no occasion of sin or scandal arose . . . . The refectory and cloister were to be better guarded from strangers than was wont, lest the good fame of the nuns should vanish hereafter more than it had already done . . . One of the great troubles against which, from the first, the archbishop had to contend was that of receiving secular women to board with them." The incidents of a pregnant nun in 1346 and of visits to a local tavern in 1489 are perhaps less sinister. The Prioress in Thwates's time, who is described as "far in age" (stanza xx), had indeed died by the time of the Dissolution, or so it would seem, since the office was vacant at that time. See the *Victoria History of the County of York,* ed. William Page (London, 1913), III, 170–74.

24 Pierre Legouis, *Andrew Marvell: Poet, Puritan, Patriot* (Oxford, 1965), pp. 48–49.

25 "The masque is understood via the eye; it is 'inescapably symbolical': it is not primarily dramatic, but proceeds by presenting oppositions; design rather than plot is paramount, actors are themselves spectators; and, finally, the masque celebrates someone" (Berthoff, p. 172, n.).

But as Donald Friedman has noted, the stanzas on the meadows and woods do not suggest a Nature that is "orderly and near."[26] The severe disorder that seems, at least for a while, to overwhelm the estate, and Marvell with it, is set in contrast to both the limited order achieved by Fairfax in his architecture and gardens and the greater order imposed by Maria on all the properties of the estate. For Fairfax's influence on England has been drastically reduced by his retirement, a fact which nags at Marvell; and even the set piece on the relationship of Appleton to its neighbors (stanza ix), and the floral assault upon Cawood Castle, do not muffle the faint but distinct implications of a trivialized life, one that does not fulfill the promise of the hill that strove to raise the plain. The role of Maria, herself a Fairfax of course, thus becomes of great importance, especially in its position on the far side of Marvell's survey of the lands of the estate.

The poet's disorienting trip through the meadows and woods is, in a personal sense, a voyage of discovery. It is also an effort to come to grips with the larger terms implied by the dichotomy of Appleton versus England and order versus chaos. The masque of the harvest dramatizes the necessary savagery of Nature and its periodic reordering through the rhythms of cultivation and the mechanisms of agriculture. Viewed as though after the fact (and thus both involved and detached, empathic and ironic), the experience has the force of a nightmare rationalized in the telling, and it seeks to gain our assent to the necessity of life that feeds on death. At the vital heart of the estate, its fields, we find the cycle of labor, pain, death, and renewal characteristic of the iron

26 "The Country House Pastoral," *Marvell's Pastoral Art* (Berkeley and Los Angeles, 1970).

postlapsarian world, transforming Appleton from the somewhat toylike retreat of Fairfax's house and flower-beds into an epitome of all Nature—as suggested, in fact, by the image of the floods that erase evidence of the harvest: "The World when first created sure / Was such a Table rase and pure" (lines 445–46).

The "suttle nun" argued that the convent walls of Nunappleton afforded a liberty greater than that found outside. Within the country-house genre, the concept of the estate as an epitome is always implicit, and the frictionless dynamics of estate life imply that the enclosed area is a "paradise," as Marvell calls Appleton, in its double sense of garden and Eden.[27] The implications of seeking to impose order upon such an area are, as Marvell's survey shows, more frightening than house and gardens would suggest. The more serious task of recreating the golden world at Appleton devolves upon Maria; the importance of her special relationship with Nature is by now apparent.

The Elevation of the Estate

During his private meditations in the woods (stanzas lxi–lxxxi), Marvell mentions that

> The double Wood of ancient Stocks
> Link'd in so thick, an Union locks,
> It like two *Pedigrees* appears,
> On one hand *Fairfax,* th' other *Veres.*
> (lines 489–92)

27 See A. Bartlett Giamatti, *The Earthly Paradise and the Renaissance Epic* (Princeton, 1966), pp. 11–15.

Thus are echoed his similar expression of praise in the Bilborow poem, and the passage on Sidney's oak in "To Penshurst" (lines 13–16). Consistently with the other religious imagery of the poem Marvell, continuing the verses just cited, associates earthly glory with a divine reward: "Of whom though many fell in War, / Yet more to Heaven shooting are" (493–94). A divine reward is anticipated for Maria as well, but Marvell concentrates upon her dynastic role.

Stanzas lxxxii–lxciv return to praise of the Fairfaxes, as Marvell self-deprecatingly ends his vernal philosophizing. The general sense of his praise of Maria is clear enough: "See how loose Nature, in respect / To her, it self doth recollect" (657–58) is the text, not only of the last stanzas of "Upon Appleton House," but of other seventeenth-century compliments to women, of which Waller's poem and the Stanley translation of de Viau were perhaps Marvell's models. Maria and Nature are related by mutual influence, but the girl originates the exchange and the cycle: "'Tis *She* that to these Gardens gave / That wondrous Beauty which they have" (689–90). However, "what first *She* on them spent, / They gratefully again present" (697–98). The sun, air, waters, woods, meadows, and all the natural components of the estate bend to her, and are informed by her: "*She* streightness on the Woods bestows; / To *Her* the Meadow sweetness owes" (691–92). Maria is, in Legouis's word, the "demiurge" (p. 49) of the four elements into which the estate repeatedly resolves itself: "*She* yet more Pure, Sweet, Streight, and Fair, / Then Gardens, Woods, Meads, Rivers are" (lines 695–96).

The estate is alive; it actively responds to her, laying carpets of grass under her feet, crowning her with flowers, offering her a mirror in water but screening her from a vulgar gaze (lines 699–704). Nature in voluntary service to man, a theme both of estate poetry and of the myth of the Golden Age, is used in "Upon Appleton House" as testimony to Maria's virtue. Her moral qualities gave form to the landscape; and presumably it is her right behavior, like that of her father, that causes nature to respond to her, as the house rose to the occasion of her father's entrance (stanza vii). Like her father, Maria is righteous rather than just; she speaks in *"Heavens Dialect"* (line 712), and her *"Flames, in Heaven* try'd" (line 687) communicate a divine influence by which *"Nature* is wholly *vitrifi'd."*[28]

Maria's sights are not altogether on the next world. She has had the wisdom to avoid adolescent entanglements (stanza xc), because it is important for her to make a good match. Just as the Sidney children are extensions and continuations of their fathers, so Maria,

> . . . nurst
> Under the *Discipline* severe
> Of *Fairfax*, and the starry *Vere*,
> . . . like a *sprig of Misleto*,
> On the *Fairfacian Oak* does grow.

And for this purpose:

> Whence, for some universal good,
> The *Priest* shall cut the sacred Bud;
> While her *glad Parents* most rejoice,
> And make their *Destiny* their *Choice*.
> (lines 722–24; 739–44)

---

28 As Berthoff notes (p. 195), Maria transforms nature into a permanent and translucent structure, whereas the nun (lines 171–74) makes jam of souls.

The education of Maria in her duties is a lesser instance of the education given by her to the grounds of the estate, the "Fields, Springs, Bushes, Flow'rs" (line 745) that are directed to imitate her example (stanza xciv) and to surpass all other instances of their kind. Praise of the Fairfax family culminates in praise of the young girl, who is the future of the house. The more worldly virtues of arms, learning, and hospitality associated with both Fairfax and his daughter are subordinated in the last stanzas to the higher realities of the landscape and of heaven. Maria is conflated with earlier specimens of her line, as the prophecy of her marriage suggests: "Till Fate her worthily translates, / And find a *Fairfax* for our *Thwaites*" (lines 747–48). But her special relationship with the grounds of Appleton—and the position of these stanzas after the poet's communion with divinity in the woods—elevates both Maria and the park, with which she is particularly associated, above all other parts of the estate. As her father was praised in terms of a building, so she is understood through the medium of the natural world and, more particularly, the estate grounds, of which she is the model and pattern. Bishops-Hill, Denton, and Bilborow, Lord Fairfax's other (and presumably grander) houses, were discounted in favor of Appleton (stanza x); Tempe, Aranjuez, Bel-Retiro, and other seats of pleasure are, in a reverse pattern, "scorn'd as obsolete" (line 754) in comparison with the place where Maria walks (stanza xcv).[29]

---

29 The possibility that Statius' estate poems furnished a model for "Appleton House" rests largely on the similarity between stanza x and Statius' injunction to the Sorrentine villa (*Silvae*, II, 2) not to let itself be outdone by its master's other estates. See J. B. Leishman, *The Art of Marvell's Poetry* (London, 1966), pp. 253–57.

Earlier poets of the genre allowed gardens an extravagance that was denied to buildings; perhaps it was already implicit that the grounds of an estate could gain the first rank of prestige in a country-house poem. Marvell's idiosyncratic courtship of gardens, and the seventeenth century's pietistic veneration of nature, are of course more immediate reasons for this modification of the estate poem. Marvell conforms to the genre in linking the praise of things (natural or artificial objects) with the praise of people and fulfills his private meditations upon nature only within the generic context of praise of the masters of the house. Having elevated the grounds of Appleton by means of the animating influence of Maria, he turns at last in direct address to the property, making his well-known observation that the landscape of Appleton epitomizes nature, distilling its best qualities to their prelapsarian purity:

> 'Tis not, what once it was, the *World;*
> But a rude heap together hurl'd;
> All negligently overthrown,
> Gulfes, Deserts, Precipices, Stone.
> Your lesser *World* contains the same.
> But in more decent Order tame;
> *You Heaven's Center, Nature's Lap.*
> *And Paradice's only Map.*
> (stanza xciv)[30]

Of the several images of enclosed places that determine the sphere of the Fairfaxes—house, convent, and garden

---

30 The question of the proper punctuation and sense of the first two lines of the stanza—i.e., whether the second line complements or contradicts the first—does not affect the general sense that the "lesser world" of Appleton reorders a previous condition of disorder.

among them—the entire estate, the "lesser World," is the last and most important to be defined. The difficult task of praising the retired life of a man whose fame lay in military exploits is met by defining the place of his retirement as the epitome of the world. Through the excursion into history, Marvell gives a parallel instance of the peculiar characteristics of the retired life. The nun understands how "things greater are in less contain'd," and her perversion of erotic and devotional impulses, "still handling Natures finest Parts" (line 178), is the foil to the education of Maria and the antithesis of the history of the Fairfaxes.

The country-house genre defines the excellence of a household in terms of productivity of the fields and the right use of their fruits; Marvell associates the fields closely with God, and shifts emphasis from the manor house to them. By distinguishing between the grounds of the estate and the world beyond, Marvell can praise both Appleton and the Fairfaxes in terms of their retirement, isolation, and elevation over what is outside. In the correspondence between Fairfax and his house and gardens, and between Maria and the more important four elements of the landscape—"Fragrant Gardens, shaddy Woods, / Deep Meadows, and transparent Floods" (lines 79–80)—Marvell returns to the myth of the voluntary harmonies of man and nature that is at the basis of the genre, and of the story of the Golden Age.

Later Estate Poems: Cotton and Pope

Marvell was not the last man to write in praise of a country estate; on the contrary, it was a great vogue during the next century. But these verses do not belong to the genre of Martial and Ben Jonson, primarily because they have little or nothing to do with the contrast between a well-run, virtuous, old-fashioned estate and its opposite. They are indeed more likely to be enthusiastic encomia of splendid new buildings, and they preserve neither the thematic elements nor the satirical edge of their predecessors. An anonymous Pindaric ode of 1679, on Belvoir Castle, is representative; somewhat like Sidonius, the poet surveys the site, the history of the estate and of the family, and the beauties of the interior.[31] The praise is not qualified by irony. A more sensible poet, Anne, countess of Winchilsea (1661–1720), wrote verses on Longleat and on her own house in Kent, Eastwell. Like the memorialist of Belvoir, she cares only for the fine and the new. The motifs of the estate-poem genre do not enter into her praise of Longleat, which, however, she calls a paradise; she praises the fountains and terraces. Her poem "Upon My Lord Winchilsea's Converting the Mount in his Garden to a Terras" reflects the Restoration conversion to classicism: "No Loame, and Lath, does now this building shame, / But graceful simetry, without is seen" (lines 52–53).[32] The title is just as indicative of the new tastes.

The most important instances of the survival of generic motifs are found in Charles Cotton and in Pope. In "Wonders of the Peak" Cotton takes a moment to praise Chatsworth, the classically remodelled house built originally by the Countess of Shrewsbury a century before. Cotton contrasts the new façades and gardens with the old, to the advantage of the new, thus (uncon-

31 "Belvoir: Being a Pindarick Ode upon Belvoir Castle, the Seat of the Earls of Rutland, made in the Year 1679," *Harleian Miscellany,* IV (London, 1745), 527–45.
32 *Poems,* ed. Myra Reynolds, Decennial Pubs. of the University of Chicago, 2nd Ser., V (Chicago, 1903), 52–55, 33–36.

sciously, I think) reversing the generic assumptions. He has come to praise, not to judge, and at times the richness of the place fills him with the sense of his own insignificance. The architectural details are interesting; Cotton dispraises the old "Ruff and Farthingale" style and patronizingly bids the "honest Rosemary and Bays, / So much esteem'd in those good Wassel days"[33] to yield to the grand formal garden. His faith in the natural superiority of the modern to the old sets him apart from the country-house poets. He nevertheless does imitate the genre in his praise of the traditional virtue of the master of the house:

> . . . the great Owner, He, whose noble mind
> For such a Fortune only was design'd.
> Whose bounties as the Oceans bosom wide,
> Flow in a constant, unexhausted Tyde
> Of Hospitality and free Access . . .
>
> (lines 1464–68)

Pope's far superior lines on hospitality fall within the country-house tradition as well. They are not found in poems celebrating estates, but in the epistles to Burlington and to Bathurst, the former done on the occasion of Burlington's publication of Palladio's designs. The epistle contains an account of a fashionable dinner in a great house: "At Timon's Villa let us pass a day, / Where all cry out, 'What sums are thrown away!' "[34] In opposing moderation and utility to extravagance and waste, Pope makes use of the moral, if not the architectural dichotomy

33 Charles Cotton, *Poems*, ed. John Buxton (London, 1958), p. 92. Subsequent citations from Cotton's poems from this edition.

34 Epistle to Burlington (lines 99–100), *The Poems of Alexander Pope*, III, ed. F. W. Bateson, ii, 2nd ed. (London and New Haven, 1961), 142–143. Subsequent citations from Pope's poems from this edition.

of the estate-poem genre. Timon's pride and ostentation
are expressed in the stately but unsatisfying meal he
provides for his guests.

A contrasting landowner seems to have a Horatian
character but English responsibilities:

> His Father's Acres who enjoys in peace,
> Or makes his Neighbours glad, if he encrease;
> Whose chearful Tenants bless their yearly toil,
> Yet to their Lord owe more than to the soil;
>
> (p. 149)

Jonson describes a similar relationship at Penshurst,
where, just as with Pope, right use of the land is the first
step to virtue. Timon, in contrast, reserves his grounds for
display, and is threatened with nature's revenge. His sin is
the familiar one:

> Another age shall see the golden Ear
> Embrown the Slope, and nod on the Parterre,
> Deep Harvests bury all his pride has plann'd,
> And laughing Ceres re-assume the land.
>
> (p. 149)

Pope, of course, recommends the architecture of
Palladio, and his objections seem to be to the style of
Vanbrugh. In the set piece on Timon's villa, however, he
does not say much to indicate that Palladian architecture
is on his mind, and he pursues the generic dichotomy
without clearly relating it to the new architecture of
Burlington, which is the inspiration of the essay. Utility
and the right use of land and nature inspire both the
praise of Palladian styles and the dispraise of an extravagant country house. Although the architectural
styles of the country-house genre have nothing to do with
Pope's models, the moral distinctions are identical. Pope

177

distinguishes between being and seeming, criticizing the empty ritual in a luxurious chapel ("Where sprawl the Saints of Verrio or Laguerre"), the beautifully bound but unread books in the study, and, in a passage recalling the statues which were *not* present in the hall at Wrest, "The rich Buffet well-colour'd Serpents grace, / And gaping Tritons spew to wash your face" (p. 148).

The Epistle to Bathurst echoes Hall's satire: "Like some lone Chartreux stands the good old Hall, / Silence without, and Fasts within the wall" (p. 106). This essay concerns the right use of riches, not country living, but Pope takes country life as a touchstone of moderation and of the proper employment of resources. A miserly squire violates the traditional obligations of his position:

> No rafter'd roofs with dance and tabor sound,
> No noontide-bell invites the country round;
> Tenants with sighs the smoakless tow'rs survey,
> And turn th'unwilling steeds another way.

In Hall's words of 1598, "house-keeping's dead," and

> Benighted wanderers the forest o'er,
> Curse the sav'd candle, and un-op'ning door;
> While the gaunt mastiff growling at the gate,
> Affrights the beggar whom he longs to eat.

Pope seems to follow Hall's Satire V, 2, where the house is similarly deserted.

Although the survival of Renaissance estate mythology ceases to be remarkable in English verse after Pope, Byron's poignant evocation of his ancestral home, Newstead Abbey, illuminates an otherwise cynical passage in *Don Juan.* Admiring the continuity of family portraits, the mixed medieval-Elizabethan architecture, and the general plenitude, Byron suggests the persistence of the *topos* of the virtuous country house—a *topos* that had in fact passed from Pope's hands to those of the novelists. Fielding's praise for the hospitality of Squire Allworthy's manse in *Tom Jones,* and the Horatian excellencies of Brambleton Hall in *Humphry Clinker,* are only two examples of the virtuous country house in English fiction. Smollett's condemnation of Squire Baynard's house in the same novel (its Elizabethan façade enclosed in a neoclassical skin) echoes Martial's critique of Bassus:

> There was not an inch of garden-ground left about the house, nor a tree that produced fruit of any kind; nor did he raise a truss of hay, or a bushel of oats for his horses, nor had he a single cow to afford milk for his tea; far less did he ever dream of feeding his own mutton, pigs, and poultry: every article of house-keeping, even the most inconsiderable, was brought from the next market-town, at the distance of five miles, and thither they sent a courier every morning to fetch hot rolls for breakfast.[35]

Coleridge's Proustian observation that our idea of time is "always blended with the idea of space"[36]—that the memory or imagination of a moment in time is irrevocably linked to its physical context—justifies the complex presence of the country house at the heart of major English novels from Austen to the present. In speaking of *Mansfield Park,* Alastair Duckworth restates the Jonsonian credo:

35Tobias Smollett, *The Expedition of Humphry Clinker,* ed. Lewis M. Knapp (London, 1966), p. 292.

36 *Biographia Literaria, with His Aesthetical Essays,* ed. J. Shawcross (Oxford, 1907), I, 87.

. . . the estate as an ordered physical structure is a metonym for other inherited structures—society as a whole, a code of morality, a body of manners, a system of language—and "improvements," or the manner in which individuals relate to their cultural inheritance, are a means of distinguishing responsible from irresponsible action and of defining a proper attitude toward social change.[37]

Conclusion

The reappearance in Pope's Epistles of motifs first used by Hall suggests that the historical changes in English country-house life throughout the seventeenth century have been less influential upon "country-house poetry" than the moral tradition, in Latin and in English verse, that insistently opposes moderation and charity to ostentation and pride. Perhaps Pope consciously archaizes the virtuous country gentlemen of the Burlington essay, but I think it more likely that he, like Jonson, synthesizes a classical norm of right conduct and the right use of one's resources with an enduring and idealized legend of the role of the English manor.

The existence of a genre implies the repetition of certain characteristics from poem to poem and poet to poet. We admire the new uses that a superior artist makes of a traditional form, but we are not surprised that within a convention a poet may choose to say the old thing in the old way. English estate poems of the Jonsonian kind are too few in number to be accused of prolonged and tedious

37 *The Improvement of the Estate: A Study of Jane Austen's Novels* (Baltimore and London, 1971), p. ix.

decadence, and the genre that is no less vital in Marvell's hands than in Jonson's does not suffer in the more workaday examples written by Carew and Herrick.

The diversity of material in the six principal poems examined here reflects an unusual literary background and poses questions of source. Martial's epigram has long been recognized as the great model for "To Penshurst"; Jonson in turn may be called the founder of the tradition in England. But even a superficial examination of the English poems reveals motifs and areas of emphasis not found in the verses to Bassus. These motifs center upon the dinners in the great hall and include the matter of hospitality and behavior to guests and dependents. Martial's interest in the charitable function of a manor is slighter than that of Jonson or Jonson's successors, and the English poets, eager to praise a good table and satirize its contrary, turn mainly to Juvenal for details of the situation.

That they should so expand upon one of the characteristics of Faustinus' farmhouse points up the wholly different and much stronger role of "housekeeping" in English society. It evidences the desire of seventeenth-century poets to express the cultural ideals of their own age within the terms of ancient, or Latin, conventions. Jonson's imitation of Epigram III, 58, is itself a way of saying that the truth of Martial is a living truth and ought to be expressed again. The reliance of English poets upon a variety of Latin sources for the themes and motifs not found, or less emphasized, in Martial expresses also the sense that the contemporary qualities, good and bad, of English country houses are of the same nature as the situations praised and criticized by the Roman poets.

The virtues and vices of the manor are in large part those of its owner: the Latin poets refer us to human behavior as the proper concern of the moralist, and their emphases guide the English poets into defining the relationships between estate and proprietor. The Roman contribution to the English estate-poem genre is not limited to formal structure, or to the largely architectural dichotomy, but includes the ethical emphasis that ultimately assigns the virtues of an honorable manor and the vices of a House of Pride to the human beings who alone can bring about such situations. Jonson's sympathetic reworking of Martial's epigram, and his conflation with it of other Latin poetry examining the relationship of host and guest, establishes the ethical core of the English genre. With Hall's contribution, the genre acquires the characteristics that survive until Pope.

The richness and depth of the Roman contribution to the genre should suggest that the estate poets' intriguing analyses of historical conditions and architectural styles ought not to be naively accepted. Jonson and the later poets were not reporters; neither were they economic or architectural historians. The lament for *illud tempus* is not confined to industrial civilizations, nor to emerging mercantile powers like Jacobean England. Even in its specific form of criticism of the breakdown of old manorial customs, such a lament long antedates Jonson, and it remains much the same for a century after his death. Since they wrote about particular buildings, the estate poets have left us a body of opinion in favor of the architecture and customs of the late medieval and Tudor English manor and hostile to the most important and innovative architecture of their time. These structures do not constitute the beginnings of that Italianate school that is supposed to have had such a destructive influence upon the manners and customs of old England; and we must abandon, in my opinion, the attractive thesis that

Jonson speaks for a preindustrial society and is opposed to one based on the surplus wealth of capitalism.

Although the English poets, other than Carew, do not fail to insist upon human responsibility for what is good and bad on the estates they memorialize, it would nevertheless be an error to attribute to them as simple a relationship with the landscape as one finds in Martial's epigram. Both the Roman and the English poets search for a good man, and they find him in the countryside. In both instances, a genre begins in idealization of the countryside by the urbane moralist, who easily associates contemporary rural civilization with the plainer and better life of the past. Such idealization, in literature, draws upon its ultimate source, the myth of the Golden Age: both the pastures of Hesiod's golden men and the fields that are Maria's kindergarten respond, *sponte sua,* to the superior virtue of their human inhabitants. The English poems are richer because of this assumption and go beyond Martial to deeper sources in the poets who praise the Golden Age and to those who, like Vergil, link *illud tempus* with a modern farm.

The first age was golden, of course, because the men were golden. Marvell understands this premise, although most of us prefer to reverse it, going to the country because it is good and we have become bad. The persistence of faith in the healing powers of a bucolic environment is doubtless an instance of the universality of classical propositions; but one might keep in mind that the original golden world responded to human virtue and did not bring it about. The mere plainness or idleness of country life may pass for moderation or delight simply because one is away from town, and the pressure is off. "Anybody," Wilde remarked, "can be good in the country. There are no temptations there."

Index

Allen, Don Cameron, 150, 166
Apollinaris Sidonius, 17n, 135n, 150, 166
Appleton House: architecture of, 157–158; illustrations of, 157, 161. *See also* Fairfax, Lord; "Upon Appleton House"
Arcadia, 35–38
Architecture: attacked in country-house genre, identifying, 19–21, 63, 94–103, 112; defined, vs. "building," 89; defined, vs. "nature," 55–56; first English domestic, 62; Tudor-Stuart, social background for, 70, 92–93. *See also* Architecture, moral dichotomy in; Country houses; Country houses celebrated in genre; *names of individual country houses*
Architecture, moral dichotomy in: classical origins of, 7, 8, 13–14, 17, 182 *(see also names of individual Latin poets);* country-house poets on, 3–4, 46–62 *passim,* 100, 112–115, 142, 158–164 *passim (see also names of individual poems; names of individual poets);* earlier English poets on, 36–38, 43–44; estates illustrating *(see* Country houses, new, plans of; Country houses, traditional, plans of); generic motifs illustrating *(see* Estate, idealization of; Garden motif; Hall motif; Hospitality motif; Housekeeping; Praise of patron motif); structural details illustrating *(see* Country houses as private homes; Galleries, long; Hall; Prodigy houses; Windows, innovative)

Astraea, 8; Elizabeth I as, 24–25
Aubrey, John, 33
Audley End, 2, 70, 100; illustrations of, 76–77, 78; innovative elements in, 82, 88; traditional elements in, 73
Austen, Jane, generic motifs in, 179–180

Bacon, Sir Francis, 134; ideal house of, 83–88
Bacon, Sir Nicholas, 82–83
Balls Park, 100
Basilius, star-shaped lodge of, 37, 38, 65
Bassus, villa of: described, 14–15, 16. *See also* Martial, Epigram III, 58 of
Belvoir Castle, Pindaric ode on, 175
Berthoff, Ann, 162–163, 167, 167n
Blickling Hall, 96–97
Bolton, Edward, 94
Bradbrook, M. C., 149
Browne, William, 25
Burghley House, 61, 69, 103; illustration of, 66–67
Byron, George Gordon, Lord, generic motifs in, 178–179

Camden, William, 24
Carew, Thomas: compared to other genre poets, re detachment, 140–141; re hospitality, 130, 131; re idealization of estate, 144–146; Martial and, 115, 131; "To the King at his entrance into Saxham" by, 112. *See also* "To My Friend G. N., from Wrest"; "To Saxham"
Caroline style, described, 99–100

185